Prentice Hall

Health

Adapted Reading and Note Taking Guide

PEARSON

Prentice
Hall

Boston, Massachusetts
Upper Saddle River, New Jersey

Pearson Prentice Hall™ is a registered trademark of Pearson Education, Inc.
Pearson® is a registered trademark of Pearson plc.
Prentice Hall® is a registered trademark of Pearson Education, Inc.

ISBN 0-13-251054-5

10 11 12 V011 13 12 11

Contents

Contents *(continued)*

Contents *(continued)*

Contents *(continued)*

Contents (continued)

Contents (continued)

Contents (continued)

Contents (continued)

Contents *(continued)*

Name _____ Class _____ Date _____

The DECIDE Process (pp. 16–17)

There is a process, called DECIDE, that can help you make important decisions. Each letter in the word DECIDE stands for a step in the process. Use this worksheet to apply DECIDE to a decision you are facing. Use the table at the bottom of this page to record your responses to steps 2 and 3.

1. **Define the problem.**

   _____

   _____

2. **Explore the alternatives.**

   In the first column of the table, list four possible ways for solving your problem. Include "do nothing" if it is an appropriate alternative.

3. **Consider the consequences.**

   In the second column, list both positive and negative consequences. Consider what is likely to happen, not what you hope will happen. Think about the benefits and risks of each alternative.

Alternatives	Possible Consequences

The DECIDE Process (continued)

4. Identify your values.

Your values are the standards and beliefs that are most important to you. Wanting to be respected is an example of a value. So is wanting to help others. List five values you should consider while making this decision. Then identify those alternatives that are a good match for these values.

_____

_____

_____

5. Decide and act.

My decision is to _____

_____ .

The steps I need to take to act on this decision are

_____

_____ .

6. Evaluate the results.

Sometime after you act on your decision, review the results.

How did your decision work out? _____

_____

_____

How has it affected you and others?

_____

_____

What did you learn? _____

_____

What, if anything, would you do differently next time?

_____

_____

Section 1-4 *Summary*

Being a Wise Health Consumer (pp. 18–24)

Making Healthy Consumer Choices

Key Concept: Before buying a product, think about its safety, cost, warranty, and consumer testing.

• A **consumer** buys products or services for personal use.

• A **warranty** is an offer to repair or replace the product if there is a problem.

Key Concept: When you evaluate a service, you need to find out whether the person who will perform the service is qualified.

Key Concept: To evaluate health information, you need to evaluate the source of the information.

The Effects of Advertising

Key Concept: Ads can let you know what products and services are available, but they rarely provide the information you need to make wise choices.

• **Advertising** is the public promotion of a product or service.

• Six methods that advertisers use to sell their product are scientific studies, the bandwagon approach, testimonials, comparisons to other products, emotional appeals, and price appeals.

Health Fraud

Key Concept: People can avoid health fraud by carefully evaluating the claims made about a treatment or product.

• If a person tells lies to obtain money or property, the person is guilty of an illegal act called **fraud.**

• People who sell useless medical treatments or products are engaged in health fraud, or **quackery.**

Your Rights as a Consumer

Key Concept: As a consumer, you have the right to information, the right to consumer protection by government agencies, and the right to complain.

• Before you complain about a product or service, remember to identify the problem, decide on your goal, collect all necessary documents, and identify the person in charge.

• Sometimes you will need to put your complaint in writing.

Section 1-4 *Note Taking Guide*

Being a Wise Health Consumer (pp. 18–24)

Making Healthy Consumer Choices

1. List four factors you should consider before you buy a product.

   a. safety _____

   b. cost _____

   c. warrenty _____

   d. consumertesting _____

The Effects of Advertising

2. Complete the table about advertising methods.

Method	Message
a. Scientific studies	Scientific tests prove the product is effective.
b. the band wagon approach	Everyone is using the product. You should, too.
c. testimonals	The product is effective because trustworthy people recommend it.
d. comparison	The product is more effective than others.
e. emotional appeal	The product is safest for you and your family.
f. price appeal	The product gives you more for your money.

Name _____ Class _____ Date _____

Section 1-4: **Note Taking Guide** (continued)

Health Fraud

3. List four warning signs of quackery.

   a. <u>Someone claims that a product or treatment is the only possible cure for a health problem.</u>

   b. <u>People who sell useles medical</u>

   c. <u>products are engaged in health treat</u>

   d. <u>uses so lies to get money Prvadment</u>

Your Rights as a Consumer

4. Complete the flowchart with the main steps in the process of making an effective complaint. Use the sentences from the box below.

Identify the person in charge.	Collect documents.
Decide on your goal.	Identify the problem.

Making an Effective Complaint

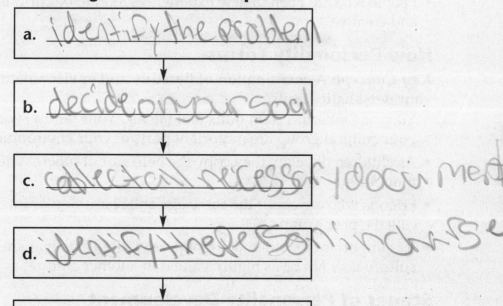

   a. <u>identify the problem</u>

   ↓

   b. <u>decide on your goal</u>

   ↓

   c. <u>collect all necessary documents</u>

   ↓

   d. <u>identify the person in charge</u>

   ↓

   e. <u>Put your complaint in writing.</u>

Section 2-1 *Summary*

Personality (pp. 30–35)

Describing Personality

Key Concept: Many researchers use five central traits to describe how people behave, relate to others, and react to change. These traits are extroversion, agreeableness, conscientiousness, emotional stability, and openness to experiences.

- Your **personality** consists of the behaviors, attitudes, feelings, and ways of thinking that make you an individual.
- A **psychologist** (sy KAHL uh jist) studies how people think, feel, and behave.
- Extroversion describes how much you like being with other people.
- Agreeableness describes your tendency to relate to other people in a friendly way.
- Conscientiousness describes how responsible and self-disciplined you are.
- Emotional stability refers to how relaxed, secure, and calm you are, even during difficult situations.
- People who are open to new experiences tend to be curious, imaginative, and creative.

How Personality Forms

Key Concept: A combination of heredity and environment influences your personality traits.

- You may inherit certain traits and talents. Your family, your friends, and your cultural group are important parts of your environment.
- As children develop, they copy the behavior of others. This is called **modeling.**
- Friends who are about the same age and share similar interests are called a **peer group.**
- It is important to remember that personality traits that are valued in one culture may not be as highly valued in another culture.

Stages of Personality Development

Key Concept: According to the psychologist Erik Erikson, personality develops throughout life as people meet a series of challenges.

- Erikson divided life into eight stages.
- Each stage presents different challenges.
- The main challenge for teens is a search for **identity,** or a sense of self.

Section 2-1 Note Taking Guide

Personality (pp. 30–35)

Describing Personality

1. Complete the table about five central personality traits.

Trait	Characteristics
a. extroversion	outgoing, talkative
b. ggreeableness	forgiving, good-natured
c. conscientiousness	dependable, organized
d. emotional stability	secure, calm
e. openness to experiences	curious, imaginative

How Personality Forms

2. Complete the concept map about how personality forms. Use the words from the box below.

family	heredity	culture	friends	environment

Personality Traits

are influenced by

a. family   b. friends

which includes

c. cultral   d. heredity   e. environmen

Section 2-1: **Note Taking Guide** (continued)

Stages of Personality Development

3. Fill in the sequence by adding Erikson's six other stages
   of personality development.

Stage

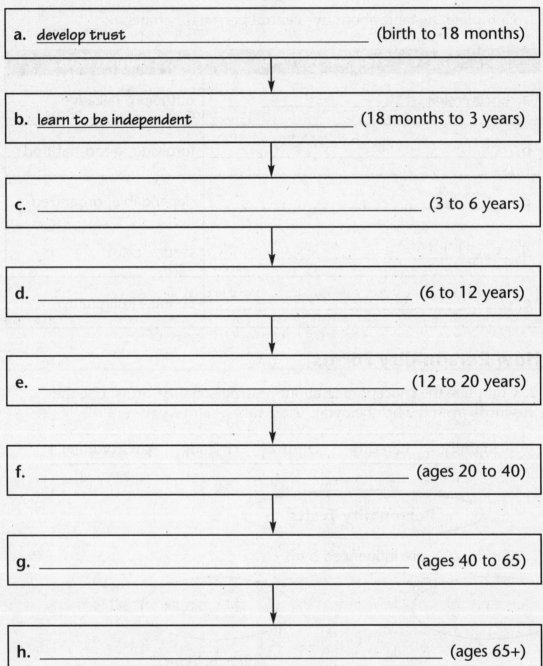

a. develop trust _____ (birth to 18 months)

b. learn to be independent _____ (18 months to 3 years)

c. _____ (3 to 6 years)

d. _____ (6 to 12 years)

e. _____ (12 to 20 years)

f. _____ (ages 20 to 40)

g. _____ (ages 40 to 65)

h. _____ (ages 65+)

Name _____ Class _____ Date _____

Chapter 2

Building Health Skills

Expressing Anger in Healthy Ways (pp. 42–43)

Some responses to anger can improve a situation or at least make you feel better. Other responses can make a bad situation worse. Use this worksheet to think about how you typically express anger and how you might respond in more positive ways in the future.

1. **Accept your feelings.**

   Explain why it is important to accept your anger.

   expresses what you like and what you don't like.

2. **Identify your triggers.**

   Before you deal with your anger, you need to know what makes you angry. Do the things on this checklist tend to make you angry?

Having to deal with certain people	Yes	No
Having to deal with certain situations	Yes	No
Thinking about events in the past	Yes	No
Thinking about my future	Yes	No

3. **Describe your response.**

   Some people tend to yell when they are angry. Some tend to cry. Some pretend they don't care. These are three possible responses to anger. Think about how you tend to behave when you are angry and record your answer below.

   I act like I don't care.

Expressing Anger in Healthy Ways (continued)

4. Seek constructive alternatives.

Which of these alternatives have you used to deal with anger?

Address the problem.	Yes	No
Release excess energy.	Yes	No
Avoid certain situations.	Yes	No
Avoid destructive behaviors.	Yes	No
Ask for help.	Yes	No

5. Evaluate your progress.

For a week, keep track of your responses to anger. Briefly describe the situation and your response. At the end of the week, evaluate your progress.

Situation	Response

Did your responses improve during the week?

_____

_____

Section 2-3 Summary

Expressing Your Emotions (pp. 44–50)

Primary Emotions

Key Concept: **Happiness, sadness, anger, and fear are examples of primary emotions.**

- An **emotion** is a reaction to a situation that involves your mind, body, and behavior.
- **Primary emotions** are emotions that people in all cultures express.
- Happiness is a normal response to pleasant events in one's life.
- Sadness is a normal response to disappointing events in your life. A period of deep sorrow is known as **grief.**
- Anger is a normal response to feeling frustrated or helpless.
- Fear is an emotion you feel when you recognize a threat to your safety or security.

Learned Emotions

Key Concept: **Love, guilt, and shame are examples of learned emotions.**

- **Learned emotions** are emotions that people express in different ways.
- Love is one of the most positive emotions people are capable of feeling.
- Guilt is an emotion you feel when you know you have done something wrong.
- Shame is an emotion that focuses on the person rather than the action.

Recognizing Your Emotions

Key Concept: **Recognizing your emotions is the important first step toward dealing with them in healthful ways.**

- When you experience a strong emotion, try to name the emotion and try to figure out what triggered the emotion.
- Then, think back to past times that you felt the same way.

Coping With Your Emotions

Key Concept: **Coping strategies are helpful when they improve a situation or allow a person to handle a situation in a better way. Coping strategies are harmful when they make a situation worse or a person is less able to handle a situation.**

- A **coping strategy** is a way of dealing with an uncomfortable or unbearable feeling or situation.
- **Defense mechanisms** are coping strategies that help you protect yourself from difficult feelings.

Section 2-3

Note Taking Guide

Expressing Your Emotions (pp. 44–50)

Primary Emotions

1. Complete the concept map about primary emotions. Use the words from the box below.

| Anger | Fear | Sadness | Happiness |

a. _____

response to pleasant events

b. _____

response to disappointment

Primary Emotions

c. _____

feeling frustrated or helpless

d. _____

normal response to a threat

Learned Emotions

2. List three learned emotions.

a. _____ b. _____ c. _____

Recognizing Your Emotions

3. Fill in the sequence for dealing with emotions in healthful ways. Use the sentences from the box below.

| Determine the trigger. | Think of similar experiences. | Name the emotion. |

Step 1

a. _____

_____

_____

Step 2

b. _____

_____

_____

Step 3

c. _____

_____

_____

Name _____ Class _____ Date _____

Section 2-3: **Note Taking Guide** (continued)

Coping With Your Emotions

4. Complete the table about defense mechanisms. Use the terms from the box below.

| Compensation | Projection | Regression |
| Rationalization | Reaction formation | Denial |

Defense Mechanism	Description	Example
a. _____ _____	refusing to recognize an emotion or problem	You act like nothing is wrong when your parents are getting divorced.
b. _____ _____	making up for weaknesses in one area by excelling in another area	You are failing two classes, but become the lead saxophone player in the band.
c. _____ _____	making excuses for actions or feelings	You steal a magazine at work because you feel like the store can afford it.
d. _____ _____	behaving in a way opposite to the way you feel	You feel guilty for bullying someone but cover your feelings by bragging.
e. _____ _____	putting your own faults onto another person	You blame your boss for firing you after you did not complete your tasks.
f. _____ _____	returning to immature behaviors to express emotions	You scream at your brother and sulk because he read your diary.

Name _____ Class _____ Date _____

Summary

What Causes Stress? (pp. 56–59)

What Is Stress?

Key Concept: You experience stress when situations, events, or people make demands on your body and mind.

- **Stress** is the response of your body and mind to being challenged or threatened.

- Positive stress is called **eustress.** Eustress may help you escape from a dangerous situation or accomplish a goal.

- Negative stress is called **distress.** Distress can have negative effects on your performance and your health.

The Many Causes of Stress

Key Concept: Four causes of stress are major life changes, catastrophes, everyday problems, and environmental problems.

- An event or situation that causes stress is called a **stressor.**

- Major life changes include both positive and negative changes. Even a positive life change, such as graduating from high school, can cause stress.

- A **catastrophe** is an event that threatens lives and may destroy property. Reading about catastrophes or seeing images on television can also cause stress.

- Everyday problems such as hassles, conflicts, and the pressure to succeed can cause stress.

- Environmental problems such as noise, unsafe conditions, or crowded conditions can cause stress.

Section 3-1 Note Taking Guide

What Causes Stress? (pp. 56–59)

What Is Stress?

Classify each situation as a source of positive stress or negative stress.

1. Pushing yourself at soccer practice _____

2. Missing practice before an important game _____

3. Not completing a homework assignment _____

4. Studying for a test _____

The Many Causes of Stress

5. Complete the concept map with examples of the different types of stressors. Use the phrases from the box below.

an earthquake	waiting in line
home is near airport	parents are getting a divorce
going away to college	a violent crime
air quality is poor	arguing with a parent

Major Life Changes

a. _____
_____

b. _____
_____

Catastrophes

c. _____
_____

d. _____
_____

Stressors

Everyday Problems

e. _____
_____

f. _____

Environmental Problems

g. _____
_____

h. _____
_____

Section 3-2 Summary

How Stress Affects Your Body (pp. 60–64)

Stages of Stress

Key Concept: The body's response to stress occurs in three stages—the alarm stage, the resistance stage, and the exhaustion stage.

- During the alarm stage, your body releases adrenaline. Adrenaline causes your heart to beat faster, your breathing to speed up, and your muscles to tense.
- Your body's first reaction to stress is called the **fight-or-flight response.**
- In the resistance stage, your body adjusts to the stressor. You may become tired and irritable.
- If the stressor continues for a long time, your body enters the exhaustion stage. You become physically and emotionally exhausted.

Recognizing Signs of Stress

Key Concept: The warning signs of stress include changes in how your body functions and changes in emotions, thoughts, and behaviors.

- It is important for your health to be able to recognize the signs of stress.
- Each person shows different signs of stress. Try to recognize your personal warning signs.

Stress and Illness

Key Concept: Stress can trigger certain illnesses, reduce the body's ability to fight an illness, and make some diseases harder to control.

- Stress can affect your health.
- Stress can bring on stomachaches, asthma attacks, and headaches.
- Stress that lasts for a long time can make you more likely to get colds or to develop heart disease later in life.

Section 3-2

Note Taking Guide

How Stress Affects Your Body (pp. 60–64)

Stages of Stress

1. Fill in the sequence about the three stages of the stress response. Use the phrases from the box below.

~~heart beats faster~~	~~muscles tense~~
~~breathing speeds up~~	~~emotional exhaustion~~
~~become tired~~	become irritable

Alarm Stage

a. adrenaline release _____

b. _____

c. _____

d. _____

↓

Resistance Stage

e. body adapts to stressor _____

f. _____

g. _____

↓

Exhaustion Stage

h. physical exhaustion _____

i. _____

Section 3-2: **Note Taking Guide** (continued)

Recognizing Signs of Stress

Classify each of the warning signs of stress listed in the box below.

sleep problems	negative thinking	increased sweating	nervous
unable to concentrate	muscle tension	irritable	overeating

2. Physical changes

   a. _____ b. _____

3. Emotional changes

   a. _____ b. _____

4. Changes in thinking

   a. _____ b. _____

5. Behavioral changes

   a. _____ b. _____

Stress and Illness

6. Complete the graphic organizer by listing some ways that stress can affect health.

Effects

Cause

Stress

a. <u>stomachaches</u> _____

b. <u>asthma</u> _____

c. _____

d. _____

e. _____

Section 3-3 **Summary**

Stress and Individuals (pp. 65–67)

Responses to Stress Vary

Key Concept: **How you react to a stressor depends on how you assess the situation.**

- People have different reactions to the same stressor. Some react with mild stress. Others show extreme stress. Still others might say that it does not bother them.

- As you assess a situation, you answer these questions:
  - Is this situation a threat to my well-being?
  - Do I have the necessary resources to meet the challenge?

Stress and Personality

Key Concept: **Your personality influences your assessment of a situation.**

- **Optimism** is the tendency to focus on the positive aspects of a situation.

- **Pessimism** is the tendency to focus on the negative and expect the worst.

- A **perfectionist** is a person who accepts nothing less than excellence. Perfectionists are never satisfied. They set goals for themselves that they can never reach.

Resilience

Key Concept: **The key factor in resilience is having the support of family and friends.**

- Some peope can tolerate high levels of stress. They tend to view stressful events as challenges, rather than as threats.

- The ability to recover, or "bounce back," from extreme or prolonged stress is called **resilience.**

Section 3-3 # Note Taking Guide

Stress and Individuals (pp. 65–67)

Responses to Stress Vary

1. What two important questions are you answering when you assess a stressful situation?

   a. _____

   b. _____

Stress and Personality

2. Complete the table about stress and personality. Use the words and phrases from the box below.

> pessimism
> optimism
> aims for perfection

Personality Trait	Description	Response to Stress
a. _____	tends to focus on the positive aspects of a situation	views situation as a challenge
b. _____	tends to focus on the negative and expect the worst	feels threatened by situation
c. _____	accepts nothing less than excellence; sets goals that are impossible to attain	tries harder, isn't satisfied, tries even harder

Name _____ Class _____ Date _____

Section 3-3: **Note Taking Guide** (continued)

Resilience

3. Use this checklist to determine how resilient you are.

a. Do you have the support of family and friends?	Yes	No
b. Do you know your strengths?	Yes	No
c. Do you make realistic plans?	Yes	No
d. Do you have good communication and problem-solving skills?	Yes	No
e. Are you able to recognize and control your emotions?	Yes	No
f. Do you recognize that change is a normal part of life?	Yes	No

Chapter 3 *Building Health Skills*

Managing Your Time (pp. 68–69)

Good time-management skills can reduce stress and help you get more done. Use this worksheet to make a plan that will help you manage your time.

1. Track how you spend your time.

In the chart, track how much time you spend on different tasks during a typical day.

Time	Task
	Eat breakfast.

2. Make a daily "To Do" list.

Break large tasks into smaller tasks that you can do in one day.

To Do List	
Do homework.	

3. Prioritize your tasks.

Rate the importance of each task according to this scale:
A = very important, **B** = somewhat important, **C** = not very important.

Managing Your Time (continued)

4. Plan your day.

Use the information from steps 1–3 to complete the table below.

Time	Task	Priority

5. Monitor your progress.

Use this checklist to monitor your progress.

Does listing your daily tasks help you get more done?	Yes	No
Does prioritizing your tasks help you decide what to do first? Do you perform "A" priority tasks first?	Yes	No
Do you refer to your list of daily tasks often?	Yes	No
Do you feel less stress and have more time to relax?	Yes	No

Section 3-4 Summary

Coping With Stress (pp. 70–76)

Take Control of Stress

Key Concept: Two techniques that can help you keep stress under control are time management and mental rehearsal.

- Some stressors, such as natural disasters, you cannot control. But you can take steps to address everyday problems.
- When you manage your time, you get more done and you feel more in control of your life.
- In a **mental rehearsal,** you practice an event without actually doing it.

Reduce Tension

Key Concept: Three strategies that can help you relieve tension are physical activity, relaxation, and biofeedback.

- Physical activity provides your body with an outlet for built-up energy and takes your mind off problems.
- Relaxation gives your mind and body a chance to rest.
- With **biofeedback,** people learn to control some body functions.

Change Your Thinking

Key Concept: One way to change your thinking is to replace negative thoughts with positive ones. You can also use humor in some stressful situations.

- Replace negative thoughts with more positive or realistic versions.
- Humor helps you deal quickly with some stressors.

Build Resilience

Key Concept: You need to build your resilience to help you deal with extreme or prolonged stress.

- There are ways to increase resilience so that you are prepared when you have setbacks in life.

Reach Out for Support

Key Concept: Sharing your problems can help you see them more clearly. Just describing your concerns to someone else often helps you understand the problem better.

- When stress becomes too much for you to handle, ask someone to help you with your problems.

Section 3-4 Note Taking Guide

Coping With Stress (pp. 70–76)

Take Control of Stress

1. Complete the graphic organizer by listing some possible results of good time management.

Cause

Good time management

Effects

a. _get more done each day_____

b. _____

c. _____

Reduce Tension

2. Use this table to organize information about methods for reducing tension. Use the terms from the box below.

biofeedback
physical activity
relaxation

Method	Goals
a. _____	provide outlet for built-up energy and shift focus from your problems to task at hand
b. _____	give your mind and body a rest
c. _____	learn to control one or more body functions affected by stress

Name _____ Class _____ Date _____

Section 3-4: **Note Taking Guide** (continued)

Change Your Thinking

3. Describe methods for changing your thinking about stressors. Use the phrases from the box below.

Find humor in a situation.   Replace negative thoughts with positive ones.
Monitor your thoughts.   Laugh at yourself.

Change Your Thinking About Stressors

Avoid Negative Thinking

a. _____

_____

b. _____

_____

Use Humor

c. _____

_____

d. _____

_____

Build Resilience

4. List strategies for building resilience.

a. <u>Take care of yourself.</u>

b. <u>Build a support system.</u>

c. _____

d. _____

e. _____

f. _____

g. _____

h. _____

i. _____

Reach Out for Support

5. Identify two ways that sharing your problems helps you.

a. <u>Helps you see problems more clearly</u>

b. _____

Section 4-1 *Summary*

Mental Disorders (pp. 82–88)

What Are Mental Disorders?

Key Concept: **Abnormal thoughts, feelings, or behaviors are symptoms of a mental disorder.**

- A **mental disorder** is an illness that affects the mind and reduces a person's ability to function, to adjust to change, or to get along with others.

Key Concept: **Physical factors, heredity, early experiences, and recent experiences can cause mental disorders.**

Anxiety Disorders

Key Concept: **Anxiety disorders include generalized anxiety disorder, phobias, panic attacks, obsessive-compulsive disorders, and post-traumatic stress disorder.**

- **Anxiety** (ang ZY ih tee) is fear caused by a source that you cannot identify or a source that is not as much of a threat as you think it is.

- When anxiety lasts for a long time and interferes with daily living, this is a sign of an **anxiety disorder.**

- Anxiety that is related to a specific event or item is a **phobia** (FOH bee uh).

- During a panic attack, a person might have rapid breathing, dizziness, and a fear of losing control.

- An unwanted thought or image that takes control of the mind is an **obsession** (ub SESH un). An obsession may lead to a **compulsion** (kum PUHL shun), a need to behave in a certain way to stop an outcome.

- People who survive or witness a life-threatening event may develop post-traumatic stress disorder.

Other Mental Disorders

Key Concept: **Some teens and young adults have mood disorders or schizophrenia. Others have impulse-control disorders or personality disorders.**

- A person with a **mood disorder** feels extreme emotions that make it hard to function well in daily life.

- A person with **depression** feels very sad and hopeless.

- A person with **schizophrenia** (skit suh FREE nee uh) has severe disturbances in thinking, mood, and behavior.

- A person with an impulse-control disorder cannot stop the drive to act in a way that is harmful to themselves or others.

- A person with a **personality disorder** has patterns of behavior that make it hard for him or her to get along with others.

Name _____ Class _____ Date _____

Note Taking Guide

Mental Disorders (pp. 82–88)

What Are Mental Disorders?

1. List three symptoms of a mental disorder.

   a. abnormal thoughts _____

   b. _____

   c. _____

2. Complete the concept map about mental disorders.

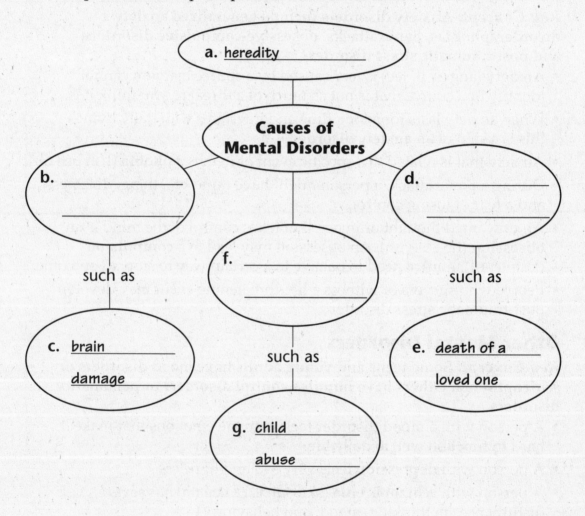

Name _____ Class _____ Date _____

Section 4-1: Note Taking Guide (continued)

Anxiety Disorders

3. Complete the table about anxiety disorders. Use the terms from the box below.

Phobia	Obsessive-compulsive disorder
Post-traumatic stress disorder	Panic attack

Disorder	Description	Warning Signs
a. _Generalized anxiety_ _disorder_	intense worry, fears, or anxiety on most days for at least six months	restlessness, fatigue, trouble sleeping or concentrating
b. _____ _____	anxiety related to a specific situation or object	dizziness, nausea, pounding heart, trouble breathing
c. _____ _____	feeling of intense fear and a desire to flee for no known reason	fast heart rate, rapid breathing, fear of suffocation, choking sensation, sweating
d. _____ _____	an unwanted thought controls the mind and may lead to a behavior to stop a feared outcome	cannot stop thinking of something, keep repeating the same action
e. _____ _____	may occur after a person survives or witnesses a life-threatening situation	flashbacks, nightmares, trouble sleeping or concentrating

Section 4-1: **Note Taking Guide** (continued)

Other Mental Disorders

4. Complete the outline by adding details about other mental disorders.

  I. Other Mental Disorders

    A. Mood disorders

      extreme emotions make it difficult to function well in daily life;

      bipolar disorder is a mood disorder in which manic episodes

      alternate with depression; a person with depression is extremely

      sad or hopeless

    B. Schizophrenia

      _____

      _____

      _____

      _____

    C. Impulse-control disorders

      _____

      _____

    D. Personality disorders

      _____

      _____

      Group A   *tend to be cold and distant* _____

      Group B _____

      Group C _____

Section 4-2 Summary

Eating Disorders (pp. 90–93)

Anorexia Nervosa

Key Concept: **A person with anorexia can starve to death. In some cases, a lack of needed minerals causes the heart to stop suddenly, leading to death.**

- An **eating disorder** is a mental disorder that involves abnormal behaviors related to food. Eating disorders are about emotions, thoughts, and attitudes.

- A person with **anorexia nervosa** (an uh REK see uh nur VOH suh) does not eat enough food to have a healthy body weight. The main symptom is extreme weight loss.

- People with anorexia often deny that they have a problem.

Bulimia

Key Concept: **Bulimia may begin in connection with a diet, but the person soon becomes unable to stop the cycle of bingeing and purging.**

- People who have **bulimia** (byoo LIM ee uh) go on uncontrolled eating binges. Then they remove the food from their bodies by vomiting or using laxatives.

- People who have bulimia are often too ashamed of their behavior to ask for help.

Binge Eating Disorder

Key Concept: **The main physical risks of binge eating disorder are excess weight gain and unhealthy dieting.**

- People with **binge eating disorder** regularly have an uncontrollable need to eat large amounts of food.

- People with binge eating disorder usually do not remove the food from their bodies after a binge.

- Some people use binge eating to avoid dealing with difficult emotions or stressful situations.

Section 4-2 *Note Taking Guide*

Eating Disorders (pp. 90–93)

Anorexia Nervosa

Bulimia

Binge Eating Disorder

1. Complete the table about eating disorders.

Eating disorder	a. _____ _____	b. _____ _____	c. _____ _____
Definition	person does not eat enough food to maintain a healthy weight	person has uncontrolled eating, followed by purging	person regularly has an uncontrollable urge to eat large amounts of food
Symptoms	extreme weight loss; growth of fine body hair; lowered body temperature	eating in private; bathroom visits after eating; cycles of weight gain and loss	eating large amounts of food in a short time; cannot stop eating even when full
Health risks	starving to death; heart stops due to lack of essential minerals	dehydration; kidney damage; eroded tooth enamel; depression	excess weight gain; unhealthy dieting; greater risk of diabetes and high blood pressure
Treatment	stop the weight loss; change eating habits; address emotional problems	must be encouraged to seek help from a mental-health professional	learn how to control eating; address underlying emotional problems

Section 4-3 *Summary*

Depression and Suicide (pp. 94–99)

Clinical Depression

Key Concept: **Depression can cause problems at school, at home, and in one's social life. If untreated, depression can also lead to substance abuse, serious behavior problems, and even suicide.**

- People with **clinical depression** may feel sad and hopeless for months. They are unable to enjoy activities that they once thought were fun.
- Signs of clinical depression include a change in appetite, sleeping patterns, and activity level.
- Other signs are feelings of hopelessness and repeated thoughts of death or suicide.
- Medication is an effective treatment for clinical depression.

Self-Injury

Key Concept: **Self-injury is an unhealthy way to deal with emotions, stress, or traumatic events.**

- One example of self-injury is cutting. **Cutting** is the use of a sharp object to purposely cut or scratch one's body deep enough to bleed.
- Self-injury can be a symptom of a mood disorder, anxiety disorder, or an eating disorder.

Suicide Prevention

Key Concept: **Mood disorders, such as depression, are a major risk factor for suicide.**

- **Suicide** is the intentional killing of oneself.
- Risk factors for suicide include a family history of suicide, having both a mental disorder and a substance abuse disorder, and feelings of hopelessness.
- **Cluster suicides** are a series of suicides that occur within a short period of time in the same peer group or community.
- If a friend describes a detailed plan for suicide, tell a trusted adult.
- If you are feeling hopeless, find an adult at home, at school, or in the community to talk to.
- You can also get help by calling a crisis center or suicide hotline.

Section 4-3 *Note Taking Guide*

Depression and Suicide (pp. 94–99)

Clinical Depression

1. List five signs of clinical depression.

   a. change in appetite _____

   b. change in sleep patterns _____

   c. _____

   d. _____

   e. _____

2. List five risk factors for depression.

   a. a parent or other close biological relative with a mood disorder

   b. _____

   c. _____

   d. _____

   e. _____

Self-Injury

3. Self-injury is an unhealthy way to cope with

   a. emotions. _____

   b. _____.

   c. _____.

4. People who self-injure

   _____ a. don't hurt themselves on purpose.

   _____ b. are trying to kill themselves.

   _____ c. tend to be proud of their behavior.

   _____ d. are trying to relieve painful feelings.

Section 4-3: **Note Taking Guide** (continued)

Suicide Prevention

5. Complete the outline by adding details about suicide prevention.

   I. Suicide Prevention

     <u>Suicide is the intentional killing of oneself.</u>_____

     A. Risk factors

       1. <u>mood disorders, such as depression</u>_____

       2. <u>a previous suicide attempt or a family history of suicide</u>_____

       3. _____

       4. _____

     B. Protective factors

       1. <u>getting treatment for a mental disorder</u>_____

       2. <u>getting treatment for abuse of alcohol or other drugs</u>_____

       3. _____

       4. _____

     C. Cluster suicides

       _____

       _____

     D. Warning signs

       _____

       _____

     E. Helping others

       _____

       _____

       _____

     F. Helping yourself

       _____

       _____

Chapter 4 **Building Health Skills**

Dealing With Setbacks (pp. 100–101)

Everyone experiences setbacks in life. It is important to be able to bounce back from a setback and move on toward your goals. Use this worksheet to think about how you typically respond to setbacks and how you might respond in a more positive way in the future.

1. **Think of a setback as an isolated event.**

   Use this checklist to evaluate how you typically respond to a setback.

I see the setback as a sign that I am a failure.	Yes	No
I let a setback in one area of my life affect other areas of my life.	Yes	No
I tell myself that I simply did not succeed at one particular thing.	Yes	No

2. **Recognize that a setback is temporary.**

   A setback often changes your immediate plans. You may get discouraged and give up your original goal. It is better, however, to view the setback as an opportunity. As you answer the questions below, think about a setback you experienced recently.

Is there a different path I can take to reach my goal?	Yes	No
Can I arrange for a second opportunity to try to reach my goal, either now or in the near future?	Yes	No
Can I modify my goal somewhat?	Yes	No

Dealing With Setbacks (continued)

3. Become aware of your "self-talk."

Pay attention to what you are thinking and saying to yourself about a setback. Turn your negative thoughts into positive thoughts. In the space below, record some negative thoughts you have felt during a setback. Then change each negative thought into a positive thought. An example is included to help you get started.

Negative Thought	Positive Thought
"I can't do anything right."	"There are many things I do really well."

4. Take action.

One key to bouncing back from a setback is to focus your energy in productive ways. Pick one of the following ways you could focus your energy. Then make an action plan to achieve your goal. Record your plan in the space below.

- Work harder to improve your current skills.
- Learn a new skill.
- Find a new interest.

_____

_____

_____

_____

_____

Section 4-4   Summary

Treating Mental Disorders (pp. 102–104)

Locating Community Resources

Key Concept: **Sometimes people don't recognize the signs of a mental disorder. Or they may have been told that, with willpower alone, they can overcome the problem. Or they might not know where to go for help.**

- The first step to recovering from a mental disorder is to realize the need for help.

- If you have a mental disorder, you should see a mental health professional for treatment.

Types of Mental Health Professionals

Key Concept: **Psychiatrists, clinical psychologists, social workers, and mental health counselors are four types of mental health professionals.**

- A **psychiatrist** (sy KY uh trist) is a medical doctor who can identify and treat mental disorders.

- A **neurologist** (noo RAHL uh jist) is a medical doctor who treats physical disorders of the nervous system. A neurologist may be asked to examine a patient to find a physical cause for a mental disorder.

- A **clinical psychologist** is trained to recognize and treat behavior that is not normal. A psychologist may help a psychiatrist identify a person's mental disorder.

- A **psychiatric social worker** helps people with mental disorders and their families accept and adjust to an illness.

- Mental health counselors may deal with specific problems or work with specific groups of people.

Kinds of Treatments

Key Concept: **Psychotherapy, drug therapy, and hospitalization are three methods used to treat mental disorders.**

- During psychotherapy, people talk with a therapist to help understand and overcome their mental disorders.

- Three types of psychotherapy are insight therapy, cognitive and behavioral therapy, and group therapy.

- Doctors may prescribe drugs to help lessen the symptoms of a mental disorder and allow people to function normally.

- Sometimes, when people with a mental disorder are in danger of hurting themselves or others, they will be treated in a hospital.

Section 4-4 *Note Taking Guide*

Treating Mental Disorders (pp. 102–104)

Locating Community Resources

1. List three reasons why people do not seek help for a mental disorder.

   a. <u>*do not recognize the signs of a mental disorder*</u>

   b. _____

   c. _____

Types of Mental Health Professionals

2. Complete the table about mental health professionals. Use the terms from the box below.

Social worker	Mental health counselor
Clinical psychologist	Psychiatrist

Mental Health Professional	Description
a. _____ _____	a physician who diagnoses and treats mental disorders; able to prescribe medications
b. _____ _____	recognizes and treats abnormal behaviors; may interview a patient or use tests
c. _____ _____	helps connect people to resources in the community
d. _____ _____	may focus on specific problems or on specific groups of people

Section 4-4: **Note Taking Guide** (continued)

Kinds of Treatments

3. Complete the outline by adding details about treatments for mental disorders.

I. Kinds of Treatments

Some disorders and some patients respond better to some

treatments than to others.

A. Psychotherapy

1. Insight therapy helps people better understand the reasons

for their behavior; with insight, people may be able to change

their behavior

2. Cognitive and behavioral therapy _____

_____

_____

3. Group therapy _____

_____

_____

B. Drug therapy

_____

_____

_____

C. Hospitalization

_____

_____

_____

Section 5-1 Summary

Families Today (pp. 112–117)

The Family and Social Health

Key Concept: If the relationships with family members are healthy, a child learns to love, respect, get along with others, and to function as part of a group.

- The family is often called "the basic unit of society" because it is where children are raised and values are learned.

The Changing Family

Key Concept: Three main factors account for changes in the American family. These factors are more women in the work force, a high divorce rate, and an increase in the age at which people marry.

- A **divorce** is a legal agreement to end a marriage. Divorce affects a family's structure, finances, and health.

Family Forms

Key Concept: Children can live in nuclear, single-parent, extended, blended, or foster families.

- A **nuclear family** consists of a couple and their child or children living together in one household. **Adoption** is the legal process by which parents take another person's child into their family to be raised as their own.

- A **single-parent family** is a family in which only one parent lives with the child or children.

- An **extended family** is a group of close relatives living together or near each other.

- A **blended family** consists of a biological parent, a stepparent, and the children of one or both parents.

- A **foster family** consists of an adult or couple who cares for children whose biological parents are unable to care for them.

- Other types of families include married couples without children or unrelated individuals who live together and care for one another.

Responsibilities Within the Family

Key Concept: Often there are some responsibilities that clearly belong to the adults, some that clearly belong to the children, and some that can be shared.

- **Socialization** (soh shuh lih ZAY shun) is the process by which adults teach children to behave in a way that is acceptable to the family and to society.

Section 5-1 Note Taking Guide

Families Today (pp. 112–117)

The Family and Social Health

1. List three things that children can learn when relationships within a family are healthy.

   a. _to love and respect others_____

   b. _____

   c. _____

The Changing Family

2. Complete the graphic organizer about the changing family. Use the phrases from the box below.

   > postponing marriage
   > more women in work force
   > high divorce rate

   Cause   **Effects**

   a. _____   →   families spend less time
      _____   together; parents must
                                              trust others to care for
                                              their children

   b. _____   →   changes in the family's
      _____   structure and finances;
                                              could affect health of
                                              family members

   c. _____   →   families are smaller; more
      _____   women have no children

Name _____ Class _____ Date _____

Section 5-1: **Note Taking Guide** (continued)

Family Forms

3. Complete the table about family forms. Use the terms from the box below.

| Nuclear family | Other families | Blended family |
| Extended family | Foster family | Single-parent family |

Types of Families	
Family Form	**Description**
a. _____	a couple and their child or children living together in one household
b. _____	only one parent lives with a child or children
c. _____	a group of close relatives living together or near each other
d. _____	a biological parent, a stepparent, and the children of one or both parents
e. _____	an adult or couple cares for children whose biological parents are unable to care for them
f. _____	a married couple without children or a group of unrelated people who choose to live together

Name _____ Class _____ Date _____

Section 5-1: **Note Taking Guide** (continued)

Responsibilities Within the Family

4. Compare adults' responsibilities and children's responsibilities by completing the Venn diagram. Write similarities where the circles overlap, and differences on the left and right sides. Use the phrases from the box below.

providing for basic needs	tidying up after self
following rules	setting rules
doing homework	socialization

Adults'
Responsibilities   **Children's**
                             Responsibilities

a. _____

  _____

b. _____

  _____

c. _____

  _____

d. <u>doing household</u>

  <u>chores</u>

e. <u>caring for other</u>

  <u>family members</u>

f. _____

  _____

g. _____

  _____

h. _____

  _____

Section 5-2 *Summary*

Family Problems (pp. 119–123)

Causes of Family Stress

Key Concept: Some sources of family stress are illness, financial problems, divorce, and drug abuse.

- When one family member has a serious illness, it affects everyone in the family.
- Serious illness, divorce, or loss of a job can lead to financial, or money, problems.
- A **separation** is an arrangement in which spouses live apart and try to work out their problems. If a couple is not able to work out their differences, a separation may lead to divorce.
- When a family member has a problem with alcohol or another drug, the whole family is affected.

Family Violence

Key Concept: Violence, or abuse, may be physical, sexual, or emotional.

- Violence can occur in all kinds of families, and any family member can be a victim of abuse.
- The abuse of one spouse by another is sometimes called **domestic abuse.**
- **Physical abuse** is intentionally causing physical harm to another person.
- When an adult uses a child or adolescent for sexual purposes, he or she commits a crime called **sexual abuse.**
- **Emotional abuse** is the nonphysical mistreatment of a person.
- **Neglect** occurs when adults fail to provide for the basic needs of children.

Runaways

Key Concept: Runaways may become ill or turn to crime. They become easy targets for people who are involved with prostitution, pornography, and drugs.

- A **runaway** is a child who leaves home without permission and stays away for at least one night, or two nights for teens 15 or older.
- Many runaways end up with no place to live and no means of support.
- Many communities have shelters and hotlines to help runaways.

Name _____ Class _____ Date _____

Note Taking Guide

Family Problems (pp. 119–123)

Causes of Family Stress

1. List four sources of family stress.

   a. <u>illness</u>

   b. _____

   c. _____

   d. _____

Family Violence

2. Complete the table about different types of abuse of children.

Type of Abuse	Definition
a. _____	intentionally causing physical harm to another person
b. _____	when an adult uses a child or adolescent for sexual purposes
c. _____	nonphysical mistreatment of a person
d. _____	when an adult fails to provide for the basic needs of children

Section 5-2: **Note Taking Guide** (continued)

Runaways

3. Complete the outline about runaways.

   I. Runaways

      A. _____

         1. violence at home

         2. emotional problems

         3. school failure

         4. think family rules are too strict

      B. _____

         1. illness

         2. turn to crime

         3. easy targets

      C. _____

         1. shelters

         2. hotlines

Name _____ Class _____ Date _____

Chapter 5   *Building Health Skills*

Using Win-Win Negotiation (pp. 124–125)

The key to resolving conflicts is to find common goals that both people share. By using "win-win" negotiation, you can turn a no-win situation into one where everyone comes out a winner. Use this worksheet to figure out how you could use "win-win" negotiation to resolve a conflict.

1. **Describe the problem.**

   List four questions you should answer when you have a conflict with someone.

   a. <u>What do you think the problem is?</u> _____

   b. _____

   c. _____

   d. _____

2. **See the other point of view.**

   Now you need to understand how the other person sees the problem. What three things should you consider?

   a. <u>thoughts</u> _____

   b. _____

   c. _____

3. **Involve the other person.**

   Describe how you can involve the other person in the "win-win" negotiation process.

   _____

   _____

   _____

   _____

   _____

© Pearson Education, Inc., publishing as Pearson Prentice Hall. All rights reserved.

60-A

Name _____ Class _____ Date _____

Use Win-Win Negotiation (continued)

4. Share and discuss.

List six things to keep in mind as you discuss the conflict with the other person.

a. <u>Listen closely and don't interrupt while the other person is talking.</u>

_____

b. _____

_____

c. _____

_____

d. _____

_____

e. _____

_____

f. _____

_____

5. Invent solutions.

What is the most important thing to keep in mind as you try to think of solutions?

_____

_____

6. Agree on a solution.

a. Which solution should you choose?

_____

_____

b. Who must agree on the solution?

_____

_____

Name _____ Class _____ Date _____

Keeping the Family Healthy (pp. 126–130)

Healthy Families

Key Concept: **Healthy families share certain characteristics: caring, commitment, respect, appreciation, empathy, communication, and cooperation.**

- People in healthy families really care about each other and are committed to staying together. They make each other feel important.

- **Empathy** (EM puh thee) is the ability to understand another person's thoughts and feelings.

- Family members communicate honestly and listen with respect to what others have to say.

- Family members share responsibilities fairly and do what they promise.

Useful Skills for Families

Key Concept: **Healthy families know how to resolve conflicts, express emotions, make decisions, and manage their time.**

- Conflict situations often involve a struggle for power.

- A **sibling** is a brother or a sister. Siblings often compete for their parent's attention, for possessions, and for recognition.

- Good communication skills and expressing emotions in constructive ways are key to resolving conflicts.

- Family members often use decision-making skills to resolve conflicts.

- If family members spend their time together wisely, they can improve their relationships.

Getting Help for the Family

Key Concept: **Some sources of help for families are family agencies, family therapists, and support groups.**

- Even healthy families may need help dealing with some problems. They may turn to relatives, friends, clergy, or mental health professionals.

- Some family agencies provide counseling for families. Others offer help in meeting basic needs.

- Family therapists work with family members to help them find better ways to solve problems.

- A **support group** is a network of people who help each other cope with a particular problem.

Section 5-3 Note Taking Guide

Keeping the Family Healthy (pp. 126–130)

Healthy Families

1. List characteristics of healthy families.

   a. <u>caring and commitment</u>

   b. _____

   c. _____

   d. _____

   e. _____

Useful Skills for Families

2. Complete the table by listing the four skills needed by healthy families. Use the phrases in the box below.

| Making decisions | Expressing emotions |
| Managing time | Resolving conflicts |

Skills for Keeping Families Healthy	
Skill	**Description**
a. _____	say what you mean, listen to others, disagree respectfully
b. _____	express emotions by focusing on your own feelings, make family members feel loved and appreciated
c. _____	think of alternatives, choose solutions that work for everyone involved
b. _____	develop family traditions, make mealtimes special, hold family meetings

Section 5-3: **Note Taking Guide** (continued)

Getting Help for the Family

3. Complete the graphic organizer about help for families. Use the terms from the box below.

Support Groups   Family Therapy   Family Agencies

Main Idea: Some sources of help for families are family agencies, family therapists, and support groups.

a. _____

may offer counseling, parenting classes, protection for children, and help with meeting basic needs

c. _____

network of people who share information and discuss their experiences with a particular problem

b. _____

work with all family members to help them find better ways to solve problems and improve family relationships

Name _____ Class _____ Date _____

Summary

Skills for Healthy Relationships (pp. 136–140)

Effective Communication

Key Concept: **Communication skills include using "I" messages, active listening, assertiveness, and using appropriate body language.**

- **Communication** is the process of sharing information, thoughts, or feelings.
- An **"I" message** is a statement that expresses your feelings, but does not blame or judge the other person.
- **Active listening** is focusing your full attention on what the other person is saying and letting that person know you understand and care.
- If you hold back your true feelings and go along with the other person, you are being **passive.**
- If you communicate opinions and feelings in a way that may seem threatening or disrespectful to other people, you are being **aggressive.**
- When you are **assertive** (uh SUR tiv), you are able to stand up for yourself while expressing your feelings in a way that does not threaten the other person.
- **Body language** includes posture, gestures, facial expressions, and body movements.
- Most Americans expect you to make **eye contact,** or meet their gaze, when you talk with them.

Cooperation

Key Concept: **Cooperation builds strong relationships that are based on mutual trust, caring, and responsibility.**

- **Cooperation** is working together toward a common goal.
- Cooperation is important in all relationships.

Compromise

Key Concept: **When you are willing to compromise, you let the other person know how important the relationship is to you.**

- **Compromise** (KAHM pruh myz) is the willingness of each person to give up something in order to reach agreement.
- There are some situations in which it is important not to compromise. Do not compromise if you are asked to do something dangerous or go against your values.

Section 6-1

Note Taking Guide

Skills for Healthy Relationships (pp. 136–140)

Effective Communication

1. Complete the table about effective communication. Use the terms from the box below.

| "I" messages | Assertiveness |
| Body language | Active listening |

Skill	Definition	Example
a. _____ _____	statements that express your feelings, but do not blame or judge the other person	"I am upset because we didn't talk last night."
b. _____ _____	focusing your full attention on what the other person is saying and letting that person know that you understand and care	nod and offer comments such as, "Then what happened?"
c. _____ _____	standing up for yourself while expressing your feelings in a way that does not threaten the other person	speak confidently and clearly
d. _____ _____	includes posture, gestures, facial expressions, and body movements	make eye contact

Section 6-1: **Note Taking Guide** (continued)

Cooperation

2. Complete the description of cooperation. Use the terms from the box below.

> responsibilities   strong relationships   common goal

   a. Cooperation is working together toward a _____.

   b. Everybody on a team must meet their _____.

   c. Cooperation builds _____.

Compromise

3. Complete the statements about when you should compromise and when you should not compromise.

Compromise when each person

   a. <u>is willing to sacrifice something.</u>

   b. _____

   _____.

You should not compromise

   c. <u>when you are asked to do something dangerous.</u>

   d. _____.

Section 6-2 Summary

Friendships (pp. 141–145)

The Importance of Friendships

Key Concept: People look to their friends for honest reactions, encouragement during bad times, and understanding when they make mistakes.

- **Friendship** is a relationship based on mutual trust, acceptance, and common interests or values.

- Most teens think it is important to be part of one or more groups of friends.

Types of Friendships

Key Concept: Some friendships are casual and some are close. Some are with friends of the opposite sex.

- Casual friendships often occur because people go to the same school, live in the same neighborhood, or have interests in common.

- People tend to form close friendships with others who share similar goals, values, or interests.

- Loyalty, honesty, empathy, and reliability are four qualities that are important in a close friend.

- **Gender roles** are the behaviors and attitudes that are socially accepted as either masculine or feminine.

Problems in Friendships

Key Concept: Some possible problems in friendships are envy, jealousy, cruelty, and cliques.

- It is normal at times to feel envy or jealousy, but if these feelings linger they can cause problems in a friendship.

- People sometimes transfer the pain or anxiety they are feeling onto their close friends by being cruel.

- A **clique** (kleek) is a narrow, exclusive group of people with similar backgrounds or interests.

- Clique members may experience **peer pressure,** a need to conform to the expectations of friends.

Name _____ Class _____ Date _____

Friendships (pp. 141–145)

The Importance of Friendships

1. List three things people look for from friends.

   a. <u>honest reactions</u> _____

   b. _____

   c. _____

Types of Friendships

2. Complete the table about qualities that are important in a close friend. Use the words from the box below.

> Honesty   Empathy   Loyalty   Reliability

Quality	Description
a. _____	A close friend sticks by you in both good times and bad.
b. _____	A close friend is truthful, even when the truth is painful.
c. _____	A close friend is caring and sensitive to your feelings.
d. _____	A close friend will try hard not to let you down.

Problems in Friendships

3. List four problems that can occur in friendships.

   a. <u>envy</u> _____   c. _____

   b. _____   d. _____

Chapter 6 Building Health Skills

Supporting a Friend (pp. 146–147)

Supporting a friend helps to strengthen the relationship. Use this worksheet to learn how to offer and ask for support.

1. Identify ways you already support your friends.

   a. List two or three ways that you support your friends.

     _____

     _____

     _____

   b. Think about other things you could do. List two ways to support friends that you have not tried yet.

     _____

     _____

     _____

2. Offer support that empowers.

   a. Describe a skill that you could teach a friend that would help the friend develop his or her own strengths and self-confidence.

     _____

     _____

   b. Describe a skill that a friend could teach you in return.

     _____

     _____

   c. List two things you could say to encourage a friend who is trying something new.

     _____

     _____

     _____

Name _____ Class _____ Date _____

Supporting a Friend (continued)

3. **Be an active listener.**

   Evaluate your skills as an active listener.

I tend to be empathetic, not judgmental.	Yes	No
I don't offer advice until a friend asks for feedback.	Yes	No
I make time to talk or do things with friends who are going through difficult times.	Yes	No
I use "I" messages to express concern when I think a friend is doing something dangerous or destructive.	Yes	No

4. **Ask your friends for support.**

   a. List two or three ways you would like to be supported by your friends. Be specific.

   _____

   _____

   _____

   _____

   b. List two things you could do to show appreciation for a friend who does something nice for you.

   _____

   _____

   _____

5. **Encourage friends to ask you for support.**

   List two ways to encourage your friends to ask for support.

   _____

   _____

   _____

Section 6-3 **Summary**

Responsible Relationships (pp. 148–151)

Physical Attraction and Dating

Key Concept: **By dating someone, you can learn about his or her personality, interests, abilities, and values.**

- Another name for feelings of intense attraction to another person is **infatuation.**
- Dating often grows out of group activities that include both males and females.
- During group activities you may discover that you especially enjoy being with a certain friend. This may lead to dating, either on your own or with other couples.
- After a few dates, a couple may decide not to date others and to see each other on a regular basis.

Violence in Dating Relationships

Key Concept: **The cycle of violence consists of a tension-building stage, a violent episode, and a calm or "honeymoon" stage.**

- **Dating violence** is a pattern of emotional, physical, or sexual abuse that occurs in a dating relationship.
- A good way to avoid the cycle of violence is to recognize the warning signs that can lead to abuse.
- More than half of the young women who are raped know the person who raped them.
- When a rape occurs during a date, the abuse is often referred to as **date rape.**
- The first step to ending an abusive relationship is to admit that the abuse exists.
- The second step is to realize that you are not to blame for the abuse.

Name _____ Class _____ Date _____

Note Taking Guide

Responsible Relationships (pp. 148–151)

Physical Attraction and Dating

Use these instructions to record details about dating.

1. List four things you can learn about a person by dating.

   a. <u>personality</u>_____   c. _____

   b. _____   d. _____

2. List two advantages of going out in a group.

   a. _____

   b. _____

3. List three factors that influence dating practices.

   a. <u>individuals</u>_____

   b. _____

   c. _____

4. List three drawbacks of steady dating.

   a. <u>limits chances to meet other people you might like</u>_____

   b. _____

   c. _____

5. List four challenges faced by teen marriages.

   a. <u>limited job skills</u>_____

   b. _____

   c. _____

   d. _____

Name _____ Class _____ Date _____

Section 6-3: **Note Taking Guide** (continued)

Violence in Dating Relationships

6. Complete the flowchart with details about each stage of the cycle of violence. Use the phrases from the box below.

makes promises	criticizes or threatens	uses force
asks for forgiveness	causes serious injury	picks fights

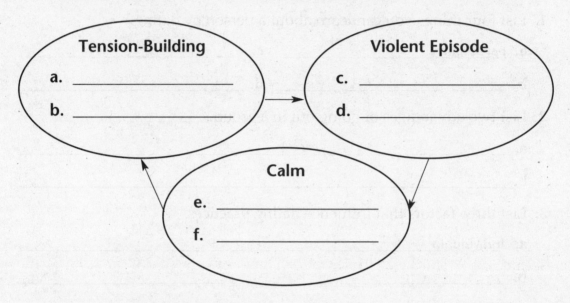

Tension-Building
a. _____
b. _____

Violent Episode
c. _____
d. _____

Calm
e. _____
f. _____

7. List five warning signs of abuse.

a. <u>Your date is jealous when you talk to others.</u>_____

b. _____

c. _____

d. _____

e. _____

8. List five tips for dating safely.

a. <u>Go out as a group.</u>_____

b. _____

c. _____

d. _____

e. _____

Name _____ Class _____ Date _____

Summary

Choosing Abstinence (pp. 152–156)

Risks of Sexual Intimacy

Key Concept: **Sexual intimacy is not risk free. The risks include the effect on your emotional health, the effect on your relationship, the risk of pregnancy, and the risk of sexually transmitted infections.**

- Decisions about sexual intimacy should be based on the values that you hold.
- Often couples are not prepared for the complications that sexual intimacy adds to their relationship.
- A teenage pregnancy can pose serious health problems for the baby and the mother.
- Some infections can be passed, or transmitted, from one person to another during sexual activity.

Emotional Intimacy

Key Concept: **A couple can have a close relationship without being sexually intimate. But it is hard for them to keep a relationship close if there is no emotional intimacy.**

- **Emotional intimacy** refers to the openness, sharing, affection, and trust that can develop in a close relationship.

Abstinence Skills

Key Concept: **Abstinence skills include setting clear limits, communicating your limits, avoiding high-pressure situations, and asserting yourself.**

- **Abstinence** is the act of refraining from, or not having, sex.
- It is important to know your limits before you go out so you can avoid having to make a hasty decision about expressing your sexual feelings.
- Once you have decided on your limits, it is important to communicate your feelings to your partner.
- You can make it easier to stick to the limits you set by avoiding certain situations.
- If you find yourself in a situation where you are not comfortable with the level of physical intimacy, don't feel guilty about saying no.

Name _____ Class _____ Date _____

Note Taking Guide

Choosing Abstinence (pp. 152–156)

Risks of Sexual Intimacy

1. Complete the graphic organizer about the effects of sexual intimacy.
   Use the phrases from the box below.

one person becomes more possessive	medical treatment throughout life
smaller, less healthy babies	can cause infertility
teen parents feel trapped	lose self-respect
affects each person's expectations	feel guilty

Possible Effects

Cause

Sexual intimacy

Effect on Your Emotional Health

a. _____

b. _____

Effect on Your Relationship

c. _____

d. _____

Risk of Pregnancy

e. _____

f. _____

Risk of Sexually Transmitted Infections

g. _____

h. _____

Name _____ Class _____ Date _____

Section 6-4: **Note Taking Guide** (continued)

Emotional Intimacy

2. List two things that can help a couple develop emotional intimacy.

   a. <u>must be honest with one another</u>

   b. _____

Abstinence Skills

3. Complete the table about abstinence skills. Use the phrases from the box below.

> Communicate your limits   Assert yourself
>
> Avoid high-pressure situations   Set clear limits

Skill	Description
a. _____ _____	consider your values and possible consequences; use DECIDE; don't let friends and media influence you
b. _____ _____	discuss things with your partner as soon as possible; talk honestly about your feelings and values
c. _____ _____	avoid unsupervised situations; avoid alcohol and other drugs; spend time with friends who share your values
d. _____ _____	speak clearly and directly; if necessary, repeat yourself; if necessary, leave; don't give in to pressure

Section 7-1 Summary

What Is Violence? (pp. 162–167)

Violence and Health

Key Concept: **With violence, there are costs to the victim, costs to the assailant, and costs to society as a whole.**

- **Violence** is the threat of or actual use of physical force against oneself or another person. Homicide, suicide, and rape are examples of violence.

- **Homicide** (HAHM ih syd) is the intentional killing of one person by another.

- Health professionals try to find ways to reduce violence.

- The **victim** of violence is the person who is attacked.

- An **assailant** (uh SAY lunt) is a person who attacks another person.

- There are financial costs and emotional costs to society connected to violence.

Risk Factors for Violence

Key Concept: **Risk factors for violence include poverty, family violence, exposure to media violence, availability of weapons, drug abuse, and membership in gangs.**

- People who don't have jobs, adequate food, healthcare, or respect from others may have a high level of frustration and anger.

- Children who witness violence or are victims of violence at home are more likely to use violence to solve their own problems.

- People's attitudes and behavior can be shaped by the violence they see on television or in movies.

- In the United States, handguns are used in most homicides and suicides.

- Alcohol and other drugs may lead to violence because they affect a person's judgment.

- **Territorial gangs** are groups that control a specific neighborhood or "turf." Most territorial gangs sell drugs and many are involved in other criminal behaviors.

Section 7-1 Note Taking Guide

What Is Violence? (pp. 162–167)

Violence and Health

1. Complete the concept map about the costs of violence. Use the terms and phrases from the box below.

| guilt | criminal charges | fear of revenge |
| emotional costs | financial costs | emotional scars |

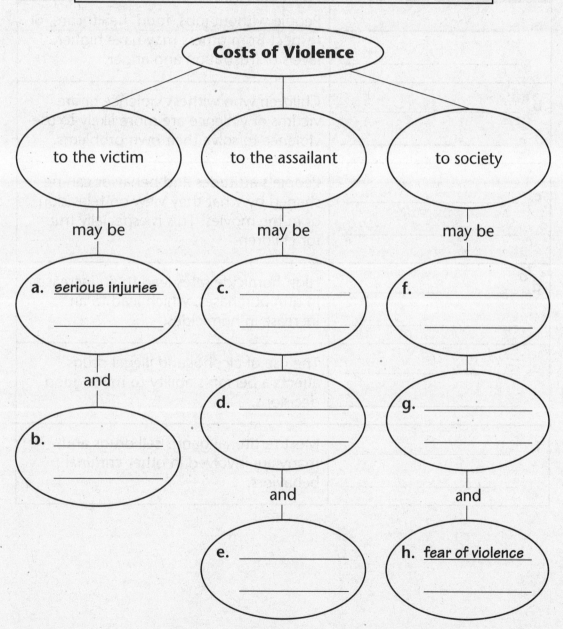

Name _____ Class _____ Date _____

Section 7-1: **Note Taking Guide** (continued)

Risk Factors for Violence

2. Complete the table about risk factors for violence. Use the terms and phrases from the box below.

Availability of weapons	Media violence
Drug abuse	Membership in gangs
Family violence	Poverty

Risk Factor	Reason
a. _____ _____	People without jobs, food, healthcare, or respect from others may have higher levels of frustration and anger.
b. _____ _____	Children who witness violence or are victims of violence are more likely to use violence to solve their own problems.
c. _____ _____	People's attitudes and behavior can be shaped by what they view on television or in the movies. This is especially true for children.
d. _____ _____	High homicide rates lead to an increase in gun purchases, which lead to an increase in homicides.
e. _____ _____	The use of alcohol and illegal drugs affects a person's ability to make good decisions.
f. _____ _____	Most territorial gangs sell drugs and many are involved in other criminal behaviors.

Section 7-2 **Summary**

Violence in Schools (pp. 168–173)

Weapons in School

Key Concept: Students who use weapons at school often are acting on the rage they feel as victims of harassment.

- **Harassment** is unwanted remarks or actions that cause a person emotional or physical harm.

Bullying

Key Concept: The most effective way to stop bullying is to get bystanders involved.

- **Bullying** is the use of threats or physical force to intimidate and control another person.
- **Cyber bullying** (SY bur) is bullying that takes place by e-mail, instant messaging, text messaging, or at Web sites.

Hazing

Key Concept: School administrators and teachers need to take the lead in the prevention of hazing.

- **Hazing** is requiring a person to do degrading, risky, or illegal acts in order to join a group.

Sexual Harassment

Key Concept: If school administrations, teachers, and students work together, they can stop sexual harassment.

- **Sexual harassment** is any uninvited and unwelcome sexual remark or sexual advance.

Hate Violence

Key Concept: The most effective way to deal with violence based on hate is through education.

- **Hate violence** is speech or behavior toward a person or group based on personal characteristics.
- **Prejudice** is negative feelings about a group based on stereotypes.
- A **stereotype** is an overgeneralization about an entire group of people.
- **Intolerance** is a lack of acceptance of another person's opinions, beliefs, or actions.
- **Discrimination** is unfair treatment based on prejudice.
- **Vandalism** is intentionally damaging another person's property.

Section 7-2 **Note Taking Guide**

Violence in Schools (pp. 168–173)

Weapons in School

1. Put a check mark in front of the correct answer.

   Unwanted remarks or actions that cause a person emotional or physical harm is known as

   _____ **a.** harassment.   _____ **c.** cyber bullying.

   _____ **b.** violence.   _____ **d.** hazing.

Bullying

2. List five ways you can help stop bullying.

   a. <u>Don't make jokes at others' expense or single out a person for exclusion.</u>

   b. _____

   c. _____

   d. _____

   e. _____

Hazing

3. Complete the graphic organizer about hazing. Use the phrases from the box below.

Preventing Hazing   Gender and Hazing

   Main Idea: Hazing is requiring a person to do degrading, risky, or illegal acts in order to join a group.

   a. _____   **b.** _____

   Male teens are more likely to report physical abuse. Females are more likely to report emotional abuse.

   School administrators and teachers need to establish rules and address reports quickly and fairly.

Section 7-2: **Note Taking Guide** (continued)

Sexual Harassment

4. Put a check mark in front of the correct answer.

   Any uninvited and unwelcome sexual remark or sexual advance is called

   _____ **a.** hazing.   _____ **c.** intolerance.

   _____ **b.** sexual harassment.   _____ **d.** discrimination.

5. List four ways you can help stop sexual harassment.

   a. <u>Speak up assertively when you feel disrespected.</u> _____

   b. _____

   c. _____

   d. _____

Hate Violence

6. Complete the table about hate violence. Use the words from the box below.

| Vandalism | Intolerance | Discrimination | Prejudice |

Action or Attitude	Definition
a. _____	negative feelings about a group based on stereotypes
b. _____	lack of acceptance of another person's opinions, beliefs, or actions
c. _____	the unfair treatment of a person or group based on prejudice
d. _____	the intentional damage or destruction of another person's property

Section 7-3

Summary

How Fights Start (pp. 174–177)

Arguments

Key Concept: **Anger is at the root of most arguments and fights.**
- The body reacts physically to anger the same way it does to stress—by preparing to fight or to run.
- If you choose to fight when you are angry, you give the other person control over you.
- Hurt pride and embarrassment often lead to fighting.

Revenge

Key Concept: **The desire for revenge leads to a dangerous cycle of fighting.**
- When revenge is the reason for a fight, the fighting can quickly **escalate,** or grow more intense.
- Revenge is a common reason for fights between territorial gangs.

Peer Pressure

Key Concept: **It is often more difficult for a person to avoid a fight when friends or bystanders are present.**
- **Instigators** are people who encourage fights between others but who stay out of the fight themselves.
- Instigators may spread rumors to bring about a conflict between people.
- Instigators may crowd around, hoping to see a fight.

Control

Key Concept: **One person's desire to have control over another is the main reason for domestic violence and dating violence.**
- Domestic violence and dating violence are growing problems in this country.
- Men can be victims of domestic violence or dating violence, but most victims are women.
- The victim is often too afraid to stay and challenge the abuser and too afraid to leave.
- There are laws to protect women in abusive relationships.
- Shelters for abused women offer legal, financial, and emotional help.
- There are also groups that try to help abusers learn to control their violent behavior.

Section 7-3
Note Taking Guide

How Fights Start (pp. 174–177)

Arguments

1. List two factors that often lead to arguments.

   a. <u>anger</u>   b. _____

Revenge

2. Complete the sentence below.

   The desire for revenge leads to a dangerous cycle of _____.

Peer Pressure

3. Describe the role of friends and the role of bystanders in fights.

   a. Friends <u>may urge you to fight while staying out of the fight themselves.</u>

   b. Bystanders _____

   _____.

Control

4. What is the main reason for domestic violence and dating violence?

   _____

   _____

5. List two reasons why a victim may not fight back.

   a. <u>fear that the violence will escalate</u>

   b. _____

Chapter 7 | Building Health Skills

Mediating a Conflict (pp. 178–179)

When two people are not able to agree on something, they may be tempted to lash out. One way to solve a conflict is to have a third person act as a mediator. A mediator can listen to what both people say. A mediator can help them find a solution that both can agree to. Use this worksheet to help you mediate a conflict.

1. **Emphasize your neutrality.**

   List three things you should tell both parties before you begin the mediation.

   a. <u>You do not have a personal interest in the outcome.</u>

   b. _____

   c. _____

2. **Establish guidelines.**

   List six rules both parties should agree on before you begin.

   a. <u>Keep everything that is said confidential.</u>

   b. _____

   c. _____

   d. _____

   e. _____

   f. _____

3. **Ask each person to state his or her view.**

   List three ways you can help both people state their views.

   a. <u>Allow each person to speak without interruption.</u>

   b. _____

   _____

   c. _____

   _____

Mediating a Conflict (continued)

4. **Identify each person's goal.**

   How should you identify each person's goal?

   <u>Try to figure out what each person cares about, which may not be what</u>

   <u>the person says he or she cares about.</u>

5. **Explore possible solutions.**

   List two ways to encourage both parties to reach a solution.

   a. When they seem relaxed _____

   _____

   _____

   _____

   b. When they are tense or hostile _____

   _____

   _____

   _____

6. **Don't give up.**

   List three tips to help reach a win-win solution.

   a. <u>Focus on what the parties agree on.</u>

   b. _____

   _____

   c. _____

   _____

Section 7-4 ## Summary

Preventing Fights (pp. 180–184)

Choosing Not to Fight

Key Concept: Once you recognize that a conflict exists, there are two general approaches you can take. You can ignore the conflict or you can confront the person.

- People need to learn peaceful ways to resolve conflicts other than fighting.
- When people who know each other fight, there is usually a series of events leading up to the fight.
- It is best to deal with a conflict before people get too angry.

Ignoring a Conflict

Key Concept: In deciding how to deal with any conflict, your safety should always be your first concern.

- In some situations, it may be smartest to walk away and do nothing at all.
- Ignoring a conflict is a sign of maturity and self-confidence.
- Learning how to control anger is an important skill.

Confronting a Person Wisely

Key Concept: To confront a person wisely, you need to choose the right time and place, stay calm, and negotiate a solution.

- Sometimes it is not possible to ignore a conflict.

Helping Others to Avoid Fights

Key Concept: You can help prevent fighting through mediation, through your role as a bystander, and by involving an adult.

- **Mediation** (mee dee AY shun) is a process for solving conflicts that involves a neutral third party.
- As a bystander, you should ignore negative remarks, refuse to spread rumors, and stay away from an area where you expect a fight will take place.
- As a friend, you can use your influence to support positive behaviors.
- If a friend reveals plans of violence to you, it is important to share those plans with a trusted adult.

Section 7-4 *Note Taking Guide*

Preventing Fights (pp. 180–184)

Choosing Not to Fight

1. Once you recognize that a conflict exists, what are two approaches you can take?

   a. _____ b. _____

Ignoring a Conflict

2. List five tips that can help you decide when to ignore a conflict.

   a. <u>You will probably never see the person again.</u>

   b. <u>The person or issue isn't very important to you.</u>

   c. _____

   d. _____

   e. _____

3. Complete the graphic organizer with details about ignoring a conflict.

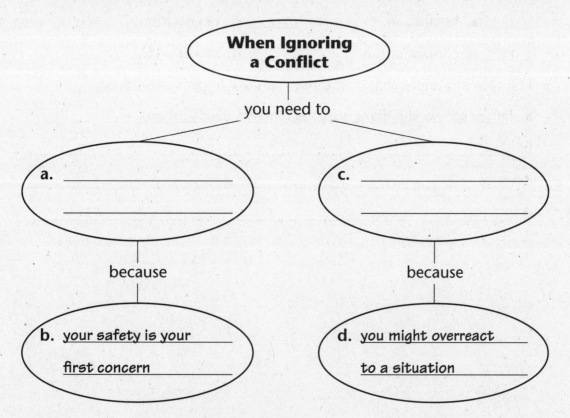

Name _____ Class _____ Date _____

Section 7-4: **Note Taking Guide** (continued)

Confronting a Person Wisely

4. Complete the flowchart with three general steps for confronting a person wisely.

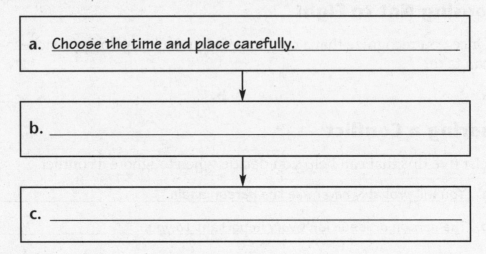

a. <u>Choose the time and place carefully.</u>

b. _____

c. _____

Helping Others to Avoid Fights

5. Put a check mark in front of the correct answer.

A process for resolving conflicts that involves a neutral third party is called a

_____ **a.** resolution.   _____ **c.** negotiation.

_____ **b.** confrontation.   _____ **d.** mediation.

6. List four strategies that bystanders can use to prevent fights.

a. <u>Ignore people who make negative remarks about others.</u>

b. _____

c. _____

d. _____

Name _____ Class _____ Date _____

Summary

Carbohydrates, Fats, and Proteins (pp. 192–199)

Foods Supply Nutrients

Key Concept: **Carbohydrates, fats, and proteins can all be used by the body as sources of energy.**

- **Nutrients** (NOO tree unts) are substances in food that the body needs. Nutrients are used to regulate bodily functions, promote growth, repair body tissues, and get energy. There are six classes of nutrients.

Foods Supply Energy

Key Concept: **When your body uses the nutrients in foods, a series of chemical reactions occurs inside your cells. As a result, energy is released.**

- **Metabolism** (muh TAB uh liz um) is the chemical process by which your body breaks down food to release energy. Metabolism also involves the use of this energy for the growth and repair of body tissues.

- The amount of energy released when nutrients are broken down is measured in units called **calories**.

Carbohydrates

Key Concept: **Carbohydrates supply energy for your body's functions.**

- **Carbohydrates** (kahr boh HY drayts) are nutrients made of carbon, hydrogen, and oxygen.

- Simple carbohydrates are also known as sugars. Complex carbohydrates include starches and fiber. **Fiber** is found in plants and cannot be digested.

Fats

Key Concept: **Fats supply your body with energy, form cells, maintain body temperature, and protect your nerves.**

- **Fats** are made of carbon, hydrogen, and oxygen, but in different amounts than in carbohydrates.

- **Unsaturated fats** have at least one bond in a place where hydrogen can be added to the molecule. **Saturated fats** have all the hydrogen atoms the carbon atoms can hold.

- **Cholesterol** (kuh LES tuh rawl) is a waxy, fatlike substance.

- **Trans fats** are made when hydrogen is added to fat in vegetable oils.

Proteins

Key Concept: **The most important function of proteins is their role in the growth and repair of your body's tissues.**

- **Proteins** contain carbon, hydrogen, oxygen, and nitrogen.

- **Amino acids** (uh MEE noh) are smaller substances that make up proteins.

Name _____ Class _____ Date _____

Carbohydrates, Fats, and Proteins (pp. 192–199)

Foods Supply Nutrients

1. Put a check mark next to the best answer.
   The body needs nutrients to

   _____ **a.** regulate bodily functions.

   _____ **b.** promote growth.

   _____ **c.** repair body tissue.

   _____ **d.** obtain energy.

   _____ **e.** all of the above.

2. Select the three classes of nutrients that supply your body with energy.

   _____ carbohydrates   _____ water

   _____ minerals   _____ fats

   _____ proteins   _____ vitamins

Foods Supply Energy

3. Put a check mark next to the correct answer.
   The chemical process by which the body breaks down food to release energy is called

   _____ **a.** nutrients.

   _____ **b.** metabolism.

   _____ **c.** nutrition.

   _____ **d.** calories.

Section 8-1: **Note Taking Guide** (continued)

Carbohydrates

4. Complete the concept map about carbohydrates. Use the words from the box below.

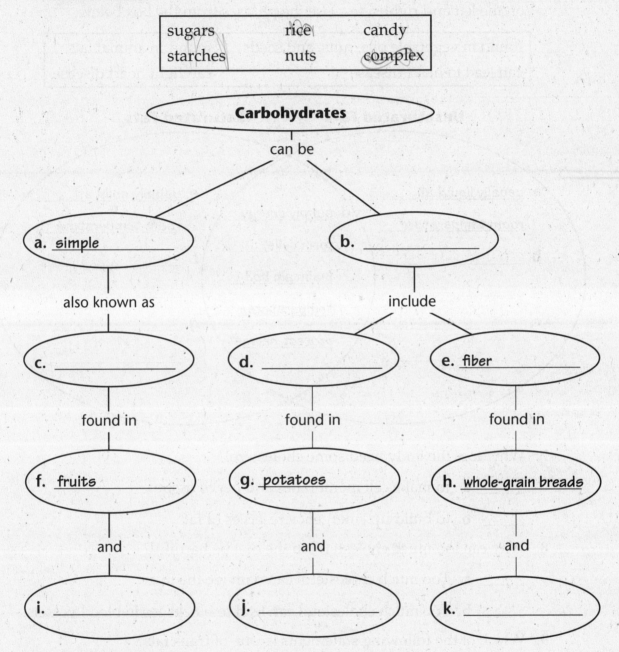

sugars	rice	candy
starches	nuts	complex

Carbohydrates

can be

a. _simple_

b. _____

also known as

include

c. _____

d. _____

e. _fiber_

found in

found in

found in

f. _fruits_

g. _potatoes_

h. _whole-grain breads_

and

and

and

i. _____

j. _____

k. _____

5. What percentage of your daily calories should come from carbohydrates?

_____ **a.** 25 to 35 percent

_____ **b.** 65 to 80 percent

_____ **c.** 45 to 65 percent

Name _____ Class _____ Date _____

Section 8-1: **Note Taking Guide** (continued)

Fats

6. Compare unsaturated and saturated fats by completing the Venn diagram. Write similarities where the circles overlap, and differences on the left and right sides. Use the phrases from the box below.

found in vegetable oils, nuts, and seeds	found in animal fats
can lead to heart disease	can fight heart disease

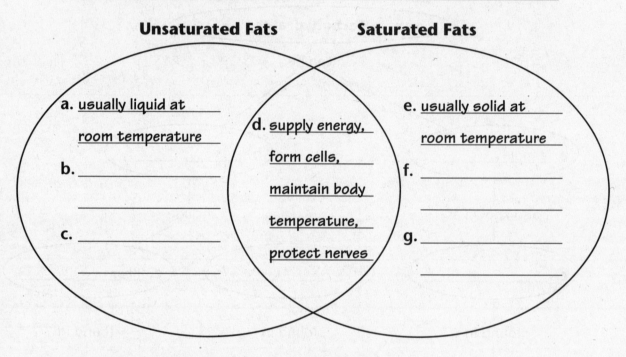

Unsaturated Fats   **Saturated Fats**

a. usually liquid at
   room temperature

b. _____

c. _____

d. supply energy,
   form cells,
   maintain body
   temperature,
   protect nerves

e. usually solid at
   room temperature

f. _____

g. _____

7. Why does the body need some cholesterol?

   _____ **a.** to make cell membranes and nerve tissue

   _____ **b.** to build up emergency reserves of fat

8. Why can too much cholesterol in the diet be harmful?

   _____ **a.** Too much cholesterol can damage the liver.

   _____ **b.** Too much cholesterol can lead to blockages in blood vessels.

9. Which of the following statements is true of trans fats?

   _____ **a.** Trans fats have many of the negative health effects of saturated fats.

   _____ **b.** Trans fats have few of the negative health effects of saturated fats.

Section 8-1: **Note Taking Guide** *(continued)*

Proteins

10. Complete the outline by adding important details about proteins.

I. Proteins

<u>Proteins are nutrients that contain nitrogen, carbon, hydrogen, and</u>

<u>oxygen. Proteins play an important role in the growth and repair of</u>

<u>the body's tissues.</u>

    A. Amino acids

<u>small units that are bound together chemically to form proteins;</u>

<u>absorbed into bloodstream and reassembled by cells to</u>

<u>form the proteins the body needs</u>

    B. Essential amino acids

_____

_____

    C. Complete and incomplete proteins

_____

_____

    D. Daily protein intake

_____

_____

    E. Proteins for vegetarians

_____

_____

Chapter 8 **Building Health Skills**

Breaking a Bad Habit (pp. 200–201)

The key to breaking a bad habit is to replace it with a new, positive habit. Use this worksheet to follow the steps that will help you break a bad habit.

1. Define the habit you want to change.

In the space below, describe the habit you want to change.

_____

_____

_____

2. Set your goal.

On the behavior contract below, identify the specific goal you want to meet and set a realistic deadline for meeting it.

Behavior Contract

Habit: _____

I _____ plan to _____

by _____ .

I will reach this goal by doing the following target behavior:

_____

_____

   To create a supportive change environment, I will get help from

the following role models: _____ , reward

myself by _____ along the way,

and by _____ when I

reach my goal.

   Signed _____ Date _____

Name _____ Class _____ Date _____

Breaking a Bad Habit (continued)

3. Design an action plan.

- Spend a week monitoring your current habit. Record your observations.

Habit Record

Beforehand		Behavior	Afterward
Scene	Feelings	Details	Results

- Summarize your action plan on the behavior contract. Your plan should be a gradual, step-by-step process.
- Keep a log of your new daily behavior, including any setbacks.

Behavior Log

Action Plan	M	T	W	Th	F	Sa	Su
	Target behavior: _____						
Behavior							

4. Build a supportive environment.

Use this checklist to help you.

Did you reward yourself for accomplishments along the way?	Yes	No
Did you ask your friends and family to keep an eye on your progress?	Yes	No
Did you keep a list of the benefits of your new behavior close by?	Yes	No
Did you structure your surroundings to support your efforts?	Yes	No

Section 8-2 **Summary**

Vitamins, Minerals, and Water (pp. 202–209)

Vitamins

Key Concept: There are two classes of vitamins. Fat-soluble vitamins dissolve in fatty materials. Water-soluble vitamins dissolve in water.

- **Vitamins** are nutrients that are made by living things and are needed in small amounts. They help in chemical reactions in the body.
- Fat-soluble vitamins include vitamins A, D, E, and K. Water-soluble vitamins include vitamin C and the B vitamins.
- **Antioxidants** are vitamins that help protect healthy cells from damage caused by aging and from certain types of cancer.

Minerals

Key Concept: You need seven minerals in significant amounts. These minerals are calcium, sodium, potassium, magnesium, phosphorus, chlorine, and sulfur.

- **Minerals** are nutrients that your body needs in small amounts. They occur naturally in rocks and soil.
- **Anemia** (uh NEE me uh) is a condition in which the red blood cells do not contain enough hemoglobin. Anemia can occur if a person is not getting enough iron.

Vitamin and Mineral Supplements

Key Concept: Vitamin and mineral supplements are not usually necessary if your diet is nutritious and well-balanced.

- If you take a vitamin or mineral supplement, take one that meets, but does not exceed, your needs. A healthcare provider can tell you how much is the right amount of a supplement to take.

Water

Key Concept: Nearly all of the body's chemical reactions take place in a water solution. The reactions include those that produce energy and build new tissues.

- Water plays an important role in homeostasis. **Homeostasis** (ho mee oh STAY sis) is the process of keeping a steady state inside your body.
- Water contains dissolved substances known as **electrolytes.** Electrolytes regulate many processes in your cells.
- **Dehydration** (dee hy DRAY shun) is a serious reduction in the body's water content.

Section 8-2 Note Taking Guide

Vitamins, Minerals, and Water (pp. 202–209)

Vitamins

1. Identify which vitamins are fat-soluble and which are water-soluble.

   a. vitamins A, D, E, and K _____

   b. vitamin C and the B vitamins _____

Minerals

2. Complete the table about minerals your body needs. Use the phrases from the box below.

baked potatoes, bananas	table salt, processed foods
maintaining heart function and water balance	formation of bones and teeth
red meats, dried fruits	

Mineral	Main Functions	Good Sources
Calcium	a. _____ _____	b. milk, broccoli, tofu _____
Potassium	c. maintaining water balance _____	d. _____ _____
Iron	e. part of red blood cells, building muscle mass	f. _____ _____
Sodium	g. _____ _____	h. _____ _____

Section 8-2: **Note Taking Guide** (continued)

Vitamin and Mineral Supplements

3. Complete the sentence below.

   Vitamin and mineral supplements are not usually necessary if

   _____ .

Water

4. Complete the outline about the role that water plays in the body.

   I. Water

   <u>Water is essential for all life processes, makes up about 65 percent of</u>

   <u>your body weight, carries dissolved waste products out of the body,</u>

   <u>and helps digest food.</u>

   A. Water and homeostasis

   _____

   _____

   B. Preventing dehydration

   _____

   _____

   C. How much water?

   _____

   _____

   D. Water versus sports drinks

   _____

   _____

Section 8-3 ## Summary

Guidelines for Healthful Eating (pp. 210–214)

The Dietary Guidelines

Key Concept: The *Dietary Guidelines* provide information on how to make smart food choices and balance food intake with physical activity. They also explain how to get the most nutrition out of the calories you eat and how to handle food safely.

- The *Dietary Guidelines for Americans* is a document that provides information to promote health. It helps people reduce their risk for heart disease, cancer, and diabetes through diet and physical activity.
- Making smart food choices involves eating a wide variety of healthy foods.
- Regular physical activity is important for overall health and fitness.
- **Nutrient-dense foods** have lots of vitamins and minerals compared to the number of calories. These foods are also low in saturated fat, trans fat, added sugar, and salt.
- Handling, preparing, and storing food safely is part of good nutrition.

The "MyPyramid Plan"

Key Concept: The MyPyramid plan differs with a person's age, sex, and activity level. The pyramid also includes physical activity as an important part of staying healthy.

- The **MyPyramid plan** groups food according to types. It tells how much of each type should be eaten daily for a healthy diet.
- The pyramid consists of colored bands that represent the food groups. The stair steps represent physical activity.

Using the Food Guidelines

Key Concept: Planning a nutritious diet does not mean that you must forego all the foods you love.

- Vary your diet at each meal. Choose healthy foods for breakfast, lunch, and dinner each day.
- When snacking or eating out, choose foods with high nutrient density.

Section 8-3 — Note Taking Guide

Guidelines for Healthful Eating (pp. 210–214)

The Dietary Guidelines

1. List four actions that the *Dietary Guidelines* recommend.

   a. <u>Make smart food choices.</u>

   b. _____

   c. _____

   d. _____

The "MyPyramid Plan"

2. Complete the outline by adding important details about the MyPyramid plan.

   I. The MyPyramid plan

   <u>a plan that groups foods according to types and indicates how much</u>

   <u>of each type should be eaten daily for a healthy diet</u>

   A. The colored bands

   <u>represent the food groups</u>

   <u>width indicates the proportion of your diet that should come from</u>

   <u>that group</u>

   B. The stair steps

   _____

   _____

   C. Creating your own MyPyramid plan

   _____

   _____

Section 8-3: **Note Taking Guide** (continued)

Using the Food Guidelines

3. Complete the graphic organizer with practical tips for following the *Dietary Guidelines* and the MyPyramid plan.

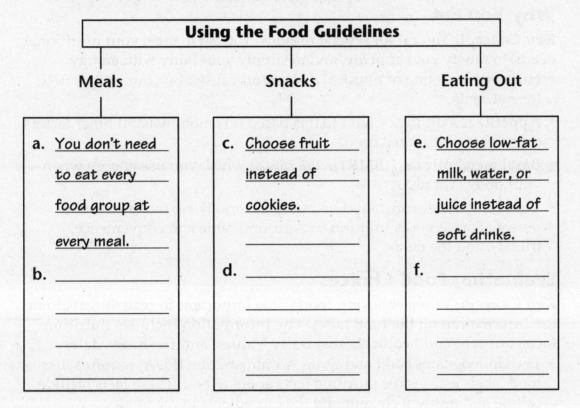

Using the Food Guidelines

Meals

a. You don't need to eat every food group at every meal.

b. _____

Snacks

c. Choose fruit instead of cookies.

d. _____

Eating Out

e. Choose low-fat milk, water, or juice instead of soft drinks.

f. _____

Section 9-1 *Summary*

Choosing Food Wisely (pp. 220–223)

Why You Eat

Key Concept: **You eat for several reasons. You eat to meet your nutritional needs, to satisfy your appetite, and to supply your body with energy.**

- **Hunger** is a feeling of physical discomfort caused by your body's need for nutrients.

- **Appetite** is a desire for food that is based on emotional and other factors rather than nutritional need.

- **Basal metabolic rate** (BMR) is the rate at which you use energy when your body is at rest.

- Your food choices are based on many factors. These factors include personal preferences, cultural background, time and convenience, friends, and the media.

Evaluating Food Choices

Key Concept: **When choosing foods, it is important to read and evaluate the information on the food label. The information includes nutrition facts, nutrient and health claims, Daily Values, and freshness dates.**

- The United States Food and Drug Administration (FDA) requires that food labels list specific nutrition facts about a food. These facts include calorie and nutrient content and the ingredients in the food.

- The FDA also sets standards about the nutrient and health claims that can be printed on a food label.

- **Daily Values** are recommendations that specify the amounts of certain nutrients that the average person should obtain each day. Food labels list the percent Daily Values for each nutrient in the food.

- Labels on prepared foods include open dates that give consumers an idea about how long the food will be fresh and safe to eat. Three kinds of dates are the "sell-by" date, the "best-if-used-by" date, and the "do-not-use-after" date.

Section 9-1

Note Taking Guide

Choosing Food Wisely (pp. 220–223)

Why You Eat

1. Complete the graphic organizer about why you eat. Use the terms from the box below.

| Appetite | Basal Metabolic Rate | Hunger |

Main Idea: You eat for several reasons: to meet your nutritional needs, to satisfy your appetite, and to supply your body with energy.

a. _____

is

A feeling of physical discomfort caused by your body's need for nutrients

c. _____

is

The rate at which you use energy when your body is at rest

b. _____

is

A desire for food based on emotional and other factors rather than nutritional need

Name _____ Class _____ Date _____

Section 9-1: **Note Taking Guide** (continued)

2. For each example, identify the factor that affects people's food choices. Use the phrases from the box below.

cultural background	personal preferences
the media	time and convenience
friends	

a. Food advertisements _____

b. A family dinner _____

c. Late for school _____

d. Eating out with peers _____

e. Love of ice cream _____

Evaluating Food Choices

3. Complete the outline by adding details about the information that is available on food labels.

   I. Evaluating Food Choices

     When choosing foods, it is important to read and evaluate the
     information on a food label.

     A. Food labels

       Food labels must list specific nutrition facts about the food,
       including calorie and nutrient content, and the ingredients.

     B. Nutrient and health claims

     _____

     _____

     C. Daily Values

     _____

     _____

     D. Open dates

     _____

     _____

Name _____ Class _____ Date _____

Chapter 9   *Building Health Skills*

Reading a Food Label (pp. 224–225)

Food labels provide important information that can help you judge the nutritional value of a food. Use this worksheet to help you analyze the information on a food label.

Nutrition Facts

Serving Size 2.5 oz.
    (70 g/about 1/3 Box)
    (Makes about 1 cup)
Servings Per Container about 3

Amount Per Serving	In Box	Prepared
Calories	260	380
Calories from Fat	25	140

	% Daily Value**	
Total Fat 2.5g*	4%	23%
Saturated Fat 1.5g	8%	20%
Trans Fat 0.5g		
Cholesterol 10mg	3%	3%
Sodium 600mg	25%	32%
Total Carbohydrate 48g	16%	16%
Dietary Fiber 1g	4%	4%
Sugars 7g		
Protein 9g		
Vitamin A	0%	15%
Vitamin C	0%	0%
Calcium	20%	25%
Iron	10%	10%

*Amount in unprepared product

**Percent Daily Values are based on a 2,000 calorie diet. Your daily values may be higher or lower depending on your calorie needs:

	Calories	2,000	2,500
Total Fat	Less than	65g	80g
Sat Fat	Less than	20g	25g
Cholesterol	Less than	300mg	300mg
Sodium	Less than	2,400mg	2,400mg
Total Carbohydrate		300g	375g
Fiber		25g	30g

INGREDIENTS: ENRICHED MACARONI PRODUCT (WHEAT FLOUR, NIACIN, FERROUS SULFATE [IRON], THIAMIN MONONITRATE [VITAMIN B1], RIBOFLAVIN [VITAMIN B2], FOLIC ACID); CHEESE SAUCE MIX (WHEY, MILKFAT, MILK PROTEIN CONCENTRATE, SALT, CALCIUM CARBONATE, SODIUM TRIPOLYPHOS-PHATE, CONTAINS LESS THAN 2% OF CITRIC ACID, SODIUM PHOSPHATE, LACTIC ACID, MILK, YELLOW 5, YELLOW 6, ENZYMES, CHEESE CULTURE)

Excellent source of calcium

1. Read the ingredients list.

   a. Which ingredient is present in the largest amount?

   _____

   b. Should a person with milk allergies avoid this product? Explain.

   _____

   _____

   _____

Reading a Food Label (continued)

2. **Note the number of servings per container.**

   a. There are _____ servings in this container.

   b. The serving size is _____ ounces.

3. **Note the number of calories in one serving.**

   a. There are _____ calories in one serving of the prepared food.

   b. There are _____ calories from fat in one serving of the prepared food.

4. **Look at the percentages of the Daily Values.**

   In the prepared product, what are the percent Daily Values for these nutrients that you should limit in your diet?

   a. Total fat _____   c. Cholesterol _____

   b. Saturated fat _____   d. Sodium _____

   In the prepared product, what are the percent Daily Values for the following nutrients?

   e. Dietary fiber _____   h. Calcium _____

   f. Iron _____   i. Vitamin A _____

   g. Total carbohydrate _____   j. Vitamin C _____

5. **Look for any health or nutrient claims.**

   Does the product advertise any health or nutrient claims on the package? If so, explain them in your own words.

   _____

   _____

   _____

   _____

   _____

Section 9-2

Summary

Safely Managing Your Weight (pp. 226–232)

What Weight Is Right for You?

Key Concept: **A person's weight is determined by various factors. Some factors include heredity, level of activity, and body composition.**

- Based on your family history, you may have a natural tendency toward a certain weight.
- The more active you are, the more calories you burn.
- **Body composition** is a measure of how much body fat you have, as compared to muscle and bone. Sex and age affect your body composition.

Body Mass Index

Key Concept: **One simple way to assess whether your weight falls within a healthy range is to calculate your body mass index.**

- **Body mass index (BMI)** is a ratio of your weight to your height.

Overweight and Obesity

Key Concept: **The number of people in the United States who are overweight is increasing. Being overweight can lead to serious health problems, including heart disease and diabetes.**

- **Overweight** describes a person who is heavier than the standard for the person's height.
- **Obesity** (oh BEE sih tee) refers specifically to adults who have a BMI of 30 or higher.
- The health risks associated with being overweight include high blood pressure, excess cholesterol in the blood, excess glucose in the blood, heart disease, stroke, and certain cancers.

Underweight

Key Concept: **Being underweight can be linked to health problems such as anemia, heart irregularities, and trouble regulating body temperature.**

- **Underweight** describes a person who is lighter than the standard for the person's height.

Healthy Weight Management

Key Concept: **Sensible weight management involves avoiding dangerous diet plans, choosing nutritionally balanced meals and snacks, and getting regular exercise.**

- Fad diets, diet aids, and fasting are unsafe ways to lose or gain weight. A **fad diet** is a popular diet that may help a person lose or gain weight without proper regard for nutrition and other health issues.

Section 9-2 ## Note Taking Guide

Safely Managing Your Weight (pp. 226–232)

What Weight Is Right for You?

1. List three factors that play a role in determining your weight.

   a. <u>heredity</u> _____

   b. _____

   c. _____

Body Mass Index

2. Complete the flowchart with the steps you should follow to calculate your body mass index (BMI).

```
┌─────────────────────────────────────┐
│              Step 1                  │
│                                      │
│  a. Multiply your height (in inches) by │
│     your height (in inches).         │
│                                      │
│  _____ │
└─────────────────────────────────────┘
                   │
                   ▼
┌─────────────────────────────────────┐
│              Step 2                  │
│                                      │
│  b. _____ │
│                                      │
│  _____ │
│                                      │
│  _____ │
└─────────────────────────────────────┘
                   │
                   ▼
┌─────────────────────────────────────┐
│              Step 3                  │
│                                      │
│  c. _____ │
│                                      │
│  _____ │
│                                      │
│  _____ │
└─────────────────────────────────────┘
```

Section 9-2: **Note Taking Guide** (continued)

Overweight and Obesity

3. List four health problems associated with being overweight.

   a. <u>high blood pressure</u>

   b. _____

   c. _____

   d. _____

Underweight

4. List three health problems that can be linked to being underweight.

   a. <u>anemia</u>

   b. _____

   c. _____

Healthy Weight Management

5. For each of the strategies listed below, decide whether it is a sensible and safe approach for losing or gaining weight. Write *weight loss, weight gain, both,* or *neither* in the space provided.

   a. fad diet _____

   b. regular exercise _____

   c. balanced diet _____

   d. skipping meals _____

Section 9-3 Summary

Nutrition for Individual Needs (pp. 233–236)

Diets for Diabetics

Key Concept: **Diabetes is a disease with dietary requirements that can help people manage their condition.**

- Poor nutritional habits and being overweight increase the risk of type 2 diabetes. Type 2 diabetes is a condition in which the blood contains high levels of glucose.

- Eating balanced meals on a regular schedule, monitoring carbohydrate intake, and controlling weight are important for managing diabetes.

Vegetarian Diets

Key Concept: **Vegetarians need to plan their food choices carefully to avoid potential health risks.**

- A **vegetarian** is a person who does not eat meat. A **vegan** is a vegetarian who does not eat any food that comes from an animal source.

- Benefits of a vegetarian diet can include a lower BMI and a lower risk of heart disease and type 2 diabetes.

- Vegetarians must plan their diets carefully to make sure that they get all the proteins, vitamins, and minerals that they need.

Food Sensitivities

Key Concept: **People with food sensitivities, which include food allergies and food intolerances, may require special diets.**

- A **food allergy** is a response by the immune system to the proteins in certain foods. Symptoms of food allergies appear suddenly and can be severe. People with allergies to certain foods should avoid those foods.

- A **food intolerance** is an inability to digest a particular food or food additive. Symptoms of food intolerance can be harder to recognize than symptoms of allergies.

Healthy Diets for Athletes

Key Concept: **Athletes need a well-balanced diet with the recommended amounts of carbohydrates, fats, and proteins.**

- Athletes need to consume extra calories to fuel their higher level of physical activity.

- Athletes should drink plenty of fluids, preferably water, to replace fluid lost in perspiration during physical activity.

- **Carbohydrate loading** is the practice of increasing carbohydrate intake and decreasing exercise on the days immediately before a competition. Carbohydrate loading is not necessary for the average athlete.

Section 9-3 **Note Taking Guide**

Nutrition for Individual Needs (pp. 233–236)

Diets for Diabetics

1. List three eating tips that diabetics should follow.

   a. <u>Eat balanced meals and snacks on a regular schedule.</u>

   _____

   b. _____

   _____

   c. _____

   _____

Vegetarian Diets

2. Complete the concept map about the health benefits and health risks of vegetarian diets.

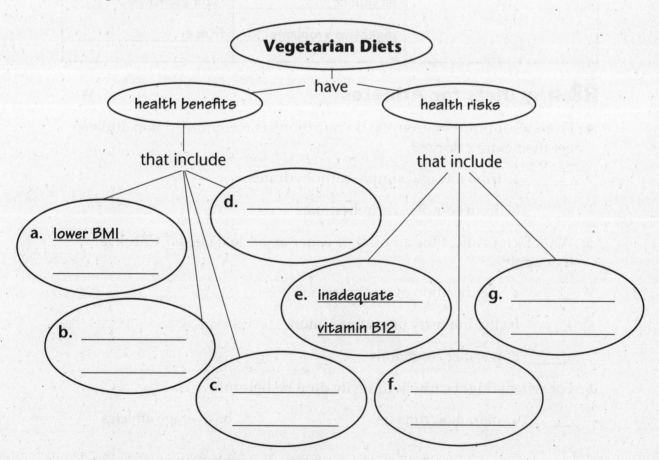

Section 9-3: **Note Taking Guide** (continued)

Food Sensitivities

3. Complete the table about symptoms and causes of food sensitivities. Use the terms from the box below.

   | Food intolerance   Food allergy |

Sensitivity	Symptoms	Common Causes
a. _____ _____	breathing difficulty coughing swelling drop in blood pressure	nuts eggs shellfish wheat
b. _____ _____	rash stuffy nose headache digestive problems	milk products chocolate food additives fruits

Healthy Diets for Athletes

4. From what nutrient group(s) do nutritionists recommend that athletes get their extra calories?

   _____ **a.** from fats and simple carbohydrates

   _____ **b.** from complex carbohydrates

5. What factors affect the amount of water an athlete needs? Check all that apply.

   _____ **a.** the duration of a competition

   _____ **b.** the intensity of a competition

   _____ **c.** weather conditions

6. For whom might carbohydrate loading be helpful?

   _____ **a.** marathon runners   _____ **b.** average athletes

Section 10-1 ## Summary

Your Digestive System (pp. 242–246)

Functions of the Digestive System

Key Concept: Your digestive system has three main jobs—to break down food, to take in nutrients from food, and to get rid of wastes.

- **Digestion** is the process by which food is broken down into molecules that the body can use.

- **Enzymes** speed up chemical reactions. Most chemicals involved in digestion are enzymes.

- During **absorption,** nutrients move through the lining of your digestive system into your blood.

- During elimination, the body gets rid of unabsorbed materials.

Structures of the Digestive System

Key Concept: The organs of the digestive system include the mouth, pharynx, esophagus, stomach, small intestine, and large intestine. The liver, gallbladder, and pancreas also are involved in digestion.

- Your teeth and tongue perform mechanical digestion in the mouth. An enzyme in saliva begins the chemical breakdown of starches. Saliva makes food moist and easier to swallow.

- Your tongue pushes food into the pharynx. The **pharynx** is the upper part of the throat where the digestive tract and the respiratory system meet.

- When you swallow, a flap called the **epiglottis** covers the opening to your windpipe. The epiglottis keeps food from going into your lungs.

- The esophagus is a muscular tube that connects the pharynx to the stomach. Waves of muscle contractions called **peristalsis** move food through the esophagus.

- In the stomach, food is mixed with acidic gastric juice. The chemical digestion of proteins begins. Food becomes a liquid called **chyme** (kym) and is released into the small intestine.

- **Bile** breaks apart large droplets of fat in the small intestine. Bile is released from a small sac called the **gallbladder.** The pancreas also releases enzymes that break down food.

- Once food is broken down, molecules are absorbed into the blood through **villi,** tiny fingerlike structures that line the small intestine.

- At the end of the small intestine, any undigested material and unabsorbed water are pushed into the large intestine. Most of that water is absorbed into the blood. Waste material forms a solid mass in the rectum and is then eliminated from the body.

Section 10-1 Note Taking Guide

Your Digestive System (pp. 242–246)

Functions of the Digestive System

1. Compare mechanical and chemical digestion by completing the Venn diagram. Write similarities where the circles overlap, and differences on the left and right sides. Use the phrases from the box below.

> breaks apart large pieces of food into smaller pieces
> breaks down food into molecules

Mechanical Digestion   **Chemical Digestion**

a. _____   b. breaks down   c. _____
_____   food   _____
_____   _____   _____
                            _____

2. What is absorption? Put a check mark next to the correct answer.

_____ **a.** process by which nutrients pass through the lining of the digestive system into the blood

_____ **b.** process by which cells get nutrients from blood

3. What does the digestive system eliminate from the body? Put a check mark next to the best answer.

_____ **a.** unabsorbed material

_____ **b.** nutrients

Name _____ Class _____ Date _____

Structures of the Digestive System

4. Complete the table about the structures of the digestive system. Use the terms from the box below.

Pharynx	Pancreas	Large intestine
Liver	Stomach	Esophagus
Gallbladder	Small intestine	

Structure	Role in Digestion
a. <u>Mouth</u>	Teeth tear, grind, and crush food. Enzymes in saliva break down starches.
b. _____	Food enters this structure after being swallowed.
c. _____	This is a muscular tube that moves food from the throat to the stomach.
d. _____	Muscles churn food and mix it with gastric juice. Enzymes start the breakdown of protein. Acid also kills bacteria.
e. _____	The chemical breakdown of food is completed. Molecules are absorbed through villi into the blood.
f. _____	This structure produces bile, which breaks up large fat droplets.
g. _____	Bile is released from this structure into the small intestine.
h. _____	Enzymes that complete the breakdown of nutrients are secreted from this structure into the small intestine.
i. _____	Remaining water is absorbed. Undigested material is eliminated.

Section 10-2 ## Summary

Keeping Your Digestive System Healthy
(pp. 248–251)

Avoiding Digestive Disorders

Key Concept: **Healthy eating habits and regular exercise are important for keeping your digestive system healthy.**

- High-fiber foods help food move through the intestines.
- Fat is digested slowly. This slow process can lead to discomfort and digestive problems.
- Overeating can strain the digestive system.
- If you relax, you are more likely to eat slowly and chew food thoroughly.
- Drink water at meals and at other times of the day.
- Regular exercise stimulates peristalsis and helps you maintain a healthy weight.

Food Safety

Key Concept: **To avoid foodborne illnesses, it is very important to prepare and store food properly.**

- **Foodborne illnesses** result from consuming a food or drink that contains poison or a microorganism that causes disease.
- Prepare and store food safely.
- Food should be cooked thoroughly.
- Uncooked foods should be kept separate from one another.
- **Cross-contamination** is the spread of microorganisms from one food to another food.
- Keep foods at proper temperatures. Quickly refrigerate leftovers. Do not defrost foods at room temperature.
- Hands and any surfaces or utensils that touched raw meat, poultry, or fish should be washed well.

Section 10-2 Note Taking Guide

Keeping Your Digestive System Healthy
(pp. 248–251)

Avoiding Digestive Disorders

1. Complete the table about healthy eating habits. Use the sentences from the box below.

Limit fatty foods.	Exercise regularly.	Drink water.
Eat when you can relax.	Eat moderately.	

Healthy Eating Habit	Benefit
a. <u>Eat plenty of fiber.</u>	helps move food through the intestines
b. _____	limits discomfort during digestion
c. _____	prevents strain on the digestive system from overeating
d. _____	helps food digest properly
e. _____	fluids help the digestive system function well
f. _____	helps keep a healthy weight

Food Safety

2. List three ways that foodborne illnesses are spread.

a. <u>when food is undercooked</u>

b. _____

c. _____

Section 10-2: **Note Taking Guide** (continued)

3. You should seek medical care if you have any of these symptoms of foodborne illness:

   a. _fever over 101.5°F_ _____

   b. _____

   c. _____

4. List four precautions you should take for proper food preparation and storage.

   a. _Cook meat, seafood, poultry, and eggs thoroughly._ _____

   b. _____

   c. _____

   d. _____

5. Which is an example of cross-contamination that can lead to foodborne illness? Put a check mark next to the best answer.

   _____ a. mixing foods together before cooking them

   _____ b. allowing food to defrost on the counter

   _____ c. cutting fruit on the same cutting board used to cut raw meat

   _____ d. leaving leftovers out on the counter for several hours

Chapter 10 *Building Health Skills*

Thinking Critically About Health News
(pp. 252–253)

Almost every day, you can find articles in newspapers and magazines, and on the Internet, that describe findings about various health topics. Is all of this information reliable? Use this worksheet as a guide to help you understand how to find out whether an article contains reliable information.

1. Who conducted the research?

During this step, you should discover who did the research and evaluate if they are qualified. Describe in your own words why you think this step is important.

_____

_____

_____

2. Is the source trustworthy?

During this step, you should evaluate where the information appeared. In the chart below, write three characteristics of a reliable source and three characteristics of an unreliable source.

Reliable Source	Unreliable Source
a. The source accepts only articles that have been thoroughly reviewed.	d. The source accepts articles that have not been thoroughly reviewed.
b. _____ _____	e. _____ _____
c. _____ _____	f. _____ _____

Thinking Critically About Health News (continued)

3. **Is the evidence convincing?**

   During this step, you should evaluate the evidence presented in the article. Identify three signs of weak evidence. For each sign, explain why it reduces the quality of the evidence.

   a. <u>Vague statements that lack supporting information are one sign. The</u>

      <u>researcher may be misleading the reader.</u>

      _____

   b. _____

      _____

      _____

   c. _____

      _____

      _____

4. **Has the information been verified?**

   During this step, you should consider findings from similar research. Explain in your own words why this step is important.

   _____

   _____

   _____

   _____

Section 10-3 ## Summary

Your Excretory System (pp. 254–258)

Organs of Excretion

Key Concept: Several organs in the body are involved in collecting and removing wastes. These organs include the liver, lungs, and skin. The major organs of excretion are the kidneys, which are part of the excretory system.

- **Excretion** is the process by which the body collects and removes wastes.
- **Urea** is a waste product made in the liver and carried by the blood to the kidneys.
- When you breathe out, your lungs exhale carbon dioxide and some water.
- Water and urea are excreted from sweat glands in the skin.
- The **kidneys** filter urea and other wastes from your blood. They also maintain water balance.
- **Urine** is a watery fluid produced by the kidneys that contains wastes.

Filtration of Wastes

Key Concept: Wastes are filtered from your blood in two steps. First, both needed materials and wastes are filtered from the blood. Then, most needed materials are returned to the blood, and the wastes are eliminated from the body.

- **Nephrons** are tiny filtering units in the kidney that remove wastes and produce urine.
- First, blood reaches a cluster of tiny blood vessels in a nephron called a **glomerulus** (gloh MUR yoo lus). Urea, salts, glucose, and some water move from the glomerulus into a capsule, and then into a tube surrounded by blood vessels.
- Second, glucose, some water, and other materials that your body needs move back into the blood. What remains in the tube is called urine.

Keeping Healthy

Key Concept: To keep your kidneys healthy, drink a lot of water. See a doctor if you have signs of an infection.

- Drinking plenty of water dilutes harmful substances that flow through the kidneys.
- Bacteria can cause infections in the urethra or bladder. Without prompt treatment, infections may spread to the kidneys.
- Kidneys can fail from injury, diabetes, high blood pressure, or disease. Kidney failure may be treated with dialysis or a kidney transplant. During **dialysis,** a machine filters blood and returns it to the body.

Section 10-3 Note Taking Guide

Your Excretory System (pp. 254–258)

Organs of Excretion

1. List four organs of excretion.

   a. <u>liver</u>_____   c. _____

   b. _____   d. _____

2. Complete the flowchart about the sequence in which urea is excreted from the body. Use the words from the box below.

bladder	ureters	liver
kidneys	urethra	

   a. Urea is produced by the _____ .

   ↓

   b. Urea is transported by blood to the _____ .

   ↓

   c. Now a part of urine, urea is collected in the _____ .

   ↓

   d. Urine is stored in the _____ until the body is ready to release it.

   ↓

   e. Urine flows out of the body through the _____ .

Section 10-3: **Note Taking Guide** (continued)

Filtration of Wastes

3. Briefly describe the two steps in which nephrons filter wastes.

   a. <u>First, needed materials and wastes are filtered from the blood.</u>

   b. _____

   _____

Keeping Healthy

4. Complete the sentences about how to keep the kidneys healthy. Use the phrases from the box below.

   | eat a low-salt diet | receive dialysis treatments |
   | take prescribed antibiotics | |

   a. To dilute harmful substances, <u>*drink plenty of water.*</u>

   _____

   b. To treat infections, _____

   _____.

   c. To prevent kidney stones, _____

   _____.

   d. To treat kidney failure, _____

   _____.

Section 11-1 **Summary**

Your Skeletal System (pp. 266–271)

Functions of the Skeletal System

Key Concept: **Your skeletal system has five main roles. It provides support, protects internal organs, allows your body to move, and stores and produces materials that your body needs.**

- Your skeleton gives your body its basic shape and provides support as you move through your day.

- Many bones protect internal organs. For example, your ribs protect your heart and lungs.

- Your skeletal system works with other systems to move your body.

Bones and Joints

Key Concept: **Your bones are living structures that undergo change throughout your life.**

- A **joint** is a place where two or more bones come together. Bones and joints work together to move the body.

- **Cartilage** is a tough, supportive tissue that is softer and more flexible than bone.

- During the process of **ossification** (ahs uh fih KAY shun) minerals are deposited within developing bone, making it hard.

- Bone consists of compact bone and spongy bone.

- **Marrow** is a tissue that fills the spaces in bones. The two types of bone marrow are red marrow and yellow marrow.

Key Concept: **Joints allow for movement and protect bones from friction and force.**

- **Ligaments** are strong, fibrous bands that hold bones together at joints.

Keeping Healthy

Key Concept: **A combination of eating well, exercising, and avoiding injuries helps keep bones and joints healthy. Regular medical checkups can help find skeletal system problems.**

- **Osteoporosis** is a condition in which bones become weak and break easily, and can occur if bones lose too much calcium and phosphorus.

- A **fracture** is a break in a bone.

- A **sprain** is an overstretched or torn ligament.

- In a **dislocation,** the ends of bones in a joint are forced out of their normal positions.

- **Scoliosis** (skoh lee OH sis) is an abnormal curvature of the spine.

Section 11-1 Note Taking Guide

Your Skeletal System (pp. 266–271)

Functions of the Skeletal System

1. List the five main roles of the skeletal system.

   a. <u>provides support</u>

   b. _____

   c. _____

   d. _____

   e. _____

Bones and Joints

2. Complete the outline by adding details about bones and joints.

   I. Bones and Joints

   A. Development of bones

   1. A newborn's skeleton is made <u>mostly of cartilage.</u>

   2. During ossification, <u>cartilage is replaced by bone.</u>

   3. After ossification, _____.

   B. Structure of bones

   1. The two types of bone tissues are _____.

   2. Red marrow produces _____.

   3. Yellow marrow stores _____.

   C. Joints

   1. Joints allow for _____.

   2. Joints protect bones from _____.

   3. Four types of movable joints are _____

      _____.

   4. Ligaments are _____.

Section 11-1: **Note Taking Guide** (continued)

Keeping Healthy

3. Complete the graphic organizer about keeping your skeletal system healthy. Use the sentences from the box below.

> Bones grow strong and dense.
>
> Get advice on preventing serious injuries.
>
> Avoid joint injuries.
>
> Maximize size and strength of bones.
>
> Avoid bone injuries.

Behavior	**Effect**
Eat foods that contain calcium, phosphorus, and other nutrients that are important for bone health.	a. _____
Get plenty of weight-bearing exercise.	b. _____
Wear appropriate safety equipment and seat belts.	c. _____
Warm up and stretch before physical activity.	d. _____
See a doctor if you experience bone or joint pain.	e. _____

Name _____ Class _____ Date _____

Summary

Your Muscular System (pp. 272–275)

The Muscles in Your Body

Key Concept: Your body has three types of muscle tissue that perform different functions—smooth muscle, cardiac muscle, and skeletal muscle.

- **Smooth muscle** is involuntary muscle that causes movements within your body. For example, smooth muscles in your blood vessels help circulate your blood.

- **Cardiac muscle** is involuntary muscle found only in the heart. Cardiac muscle allows your heart to beat and pump blood throughout your body.

- **Skeletal muscles** are the muscles that you control to do activities, such as walking. Skeletal muscles are attached to your bones.

- A thick strand of tissue called a **tendon** attaches a muscle to a bone.

- Nerves send messages to muscles commanding them to contract, or shorten and thicken, to move a bone.

- A slight tension in muscles is **muscle tone.** Muscle tone keeps your muscles healthy and ready for action.

- **Atrophy** is a condition in which muscles weaken and shrink from injury or lack of use.

Keeping Healthy

Key Concept: You can keep your muscular system healthy by exercising regularly. To help prevent injuries, exercise sessions should include a warm-up and cool-down period.

- Some types of exercise increase muscle endurance—how long a muscle can contract without tiring. Other types of exercise increase muscle thickness and strength.

- **Anabolic steroids** are artificial forms of the male hormone testosterone. Some athletes are tempted to use anabolic steroids to increase muscle size and strength. Anabolic steroids used for this purpose can damage body systems.

- A muscle **strain,** or pulled muscle, is a painful injury that occurs when muscles are overworked or stretched too much or too quickly.

- **Tendonitis** (ten duh NY tis) can occur if tendons are overused. Tendonitis can lead to painful swelling and irritation.

- Stretching and drinking lots of water before and during exercise can help you avoid muscle cramps.

Section 11-2 Note Taking Guide

Your Muscular System (pp. 272–275)

The Muscles in Your Body

1. Complete the table about muscle types.

Muscle Type	Description	Example
a. _____	involuntary muscle that causes movements within the body	smooth muscle in blood vessels
b. _____	involuntary muscle found in the heart	allows heart to beat and pump blood throughout the body
c. _____	voluntary muscle that is attached to bones by tendons	makes movement of limbs possible

2. Complete the graphic organizer about how a pair of muscles in your arm works.

Cause → **Effect**

| biceps contracts and triceps relaxes | → | a. _____ |

| biceps relaxes and triceps contracts | → | b. _____ |

3. What is *muscle tone*?

_____ a slight muscle contraction that tenses and firms the muscle

_____ a voluntary contraction that flexes and stretches the muscle

Section 11-2: **Note Taking Guide** (continued)

Keeping Healthy

4. Complete the sentences. Use the words and phrases from the box below.

strength	it increases how long the muscle can contract
endurance	it increases the muscle's size

a. Running is a type of exercise that increases a muscle's _____,

because _____.

b. Lifting weights is a type of exercise that increases a muscle's

_____, because _____.

5. Complete the table by identifying the kinds of muscle injury described.

Injury	Description	Prevention
a. _____	overworked or overstretched muscle	regular strengthening and stretching
b. _____	painful swelling and irritation of tendons	proper warm-up, rest if you feel pain
c. _____	strong, uncontrolled muscle contraction	stretching, drinking plenty of water

Name _____ Class _____ Date _____

Chapter 11

Building Health Skills

Warming Up, Stretching, and Cooling Down
(pp. 276–277)

It is important to prepare your body before you work out and after you finish. You can prepare by doing warming-up, stretching, and cooling-down exercises. Following this routine will help minimize the effects of the stress of physical activity.

Keep to the routine for one week. Use the chart on the next page to record your progress. Check off the appropriate box as you complete each part of your workout. Note which activity you perform each exercise day. Be sure to note how you feel every day, even if it is not an exercise day.

1. **Warming up** Before you exercise, warm up for the activity by starting at a reduced pace. For example, before running you could walk or jog slowly. The slow movement prepares your muscles for more intense activity.

2. **Stretching** Once you have warmed up your muscles, stretch them. You could use the stretches described on page 277 or other stretches recommended by your coach, physical education teacher, or a trainer.

   - **Lower back curl** Use the lower back curl shown on page 277 to stretch your lower back muscles in a stress-free manner.

   - **Side stretch** Perform the side stretch shown on page 277 in your text.

   - **Hamstring stretch** The hamstrings work hard in almost any exercise. Stretch them out well before you begin any activity.

   - **Calf stretch** The stride position stretches your calf muscles. The stride position is also good for stretching muscles in your shin area.

   - **Triceps stretch** Stretch your triceps as shown on page 277.

3. **Cooling down** As your workout is ending, start slowing down your rate of activity before you stop exercising. Then stretch your muscles as you did before the workout.

4. After a week, review your chart. On the lines below, write down any benefits of warming up, stretching, and cooling down that you noticed.

_____

_____

_____

_____

Name _____ Class _____ Date _____

Warming Up, Stretching, and Cooling Down (continued)

Exercise	Mon.	Tues.	Wed.	Thurs.	Fri.	Sat.	Sun.
Warm-up							
Stretching exercises							
Activity							
Cool-down							
Stretching exercises							
Notes							

Section 11-3
Summary

Your Nervous System (pp. 278–286)

What Is the Nervous System?

Key Concept: Your nervous system receives information about what is going on inside and outside of your body. Then it processes the information and forms a response to it.

• A **neuron** (NOOR ahn) is the basic unit of the nervous system.

Key Concept: Neurons carry messages, or impulses, from one part of your body to another.

• A neuron has three basic parts: dendrites, a cell body, and an axon.

• Your body has sensory neurons, interneurons, and motor neurons.

Central Nervous System

Key Concept: The central nervous system is the control center of the body. It includes the brain and spinal cord.

• The **cerebrum** controls memory, communication, and reasoning.

• The **cerebellum** (sehr uh BEL um) coordinates movements and balance.

• The **brain stem** controls involuntary actions, such as breathing and sneezing.

• The **spinal cord** is a thick column of nerve tissue that links the brain to most of the nerves in the peripheral nervous system.

• A **reflex** is a type of automatic response to your environment.

Peripheral Nervous System

Key Concept: The peripheral nervous system includes the network of nerves that links the rest of your body to your brain and spinal cord.

• The peripheral nervous system carries information to the central nervous system, and carries responses back to the body.

Keeping Healthy

Key Concept: The most important step you can take to care for your nervous system is to protect it from injury.

• A bruiselike injury to the brain is called a **concussion.**

• A **coma** is an extended period of deep unconsciousness. A coma can be caused by a severe brain injury from trauma, disease, or drugs.

• **Paralysis** is the loss of the ability to move and feel some part of the body.

• **Meningitis** (men in JY tis) causes inflammation of the membranes surrounding the brain and spinal cord.

• A **seizure** can happen when the brain experiences sudden, uncontrolled nerve impulses. People with **epilepsy** are prone to seizures.

Section 11-3 *Note Taking Guide*

Your Nervous System (pp. 278–286)

What Is the Nervous System?

1. Describe the function of each type of neuron.

   a. Sensory neurons <u>gather information about your environment.</u>

   b. Interneurons _____.

   c. Motor neurons _____.

Central Nervous System

2. Describe the function of each major region of the brain.

   a. Cerebrum <u>controls movement, memory, communication, and reasoning.</u>

   b. Cerebellum _____.

   c. Brain Stem _____.

3. Identify the main steps of a reflex action.

   ┌─────────────────────────┐
   │   You touch a hot pan.   │
   └─────────────────────────┘

   a. <u>Sensory neurons send impulses to the spinal cord.</u>
   _____

   b. _____
   _____

   c. _____
   _____

   d. _____
   _____

   ┌──────────────┐
   │ Messages of │
   │ pain travel to │
   │ the brain   │
   └──────────────┘

Section 11-3: **Note Taking Guide** (continued)

Peripheral Nervous System

4. Complete the concept map with details about the peripheral nervous system.

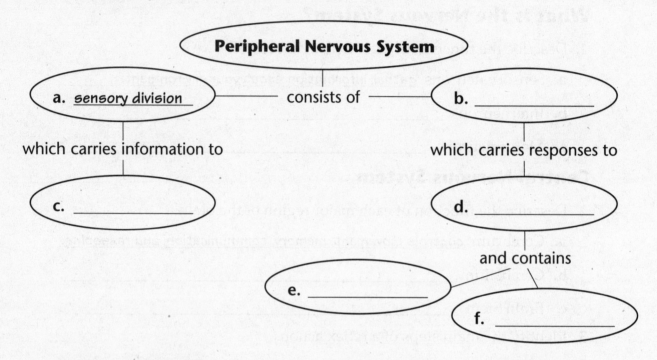

Keeping Healthy

5. Complete the table about ways to prevent nervous system injuries and diseases.

Injury or Disease	Prevention
Concussion or coma	a. wear a seat belt and a helmet when needed; avoid drugs
Paralysis	b.
Carpal tunnel syndrome	c.
Meningitis	d.
Headaches	e.

Name _____ Class _____ Date _____

Summary

Your Cardiovascular System (pp. 292–298)

Functions of the Cardiovascular System

Key Concept: **The main functions of the cardiovascular system include delivering materials to cells and carrying wastes away. In addition, blood contains cells that fight disease.**

- The cardiovascular system includes the heart, blood vessels, and blood.

The Heart

Key Concept: **The atria receive blood entering the heart. Blood flows from the atria to the ventricles, which pump blood out of the heart.**

- Each side of the heart is made up of an upper chamber called an **atrium** (plural, *atria*) and a lower chamber called a **ventricle.**

- Blood flows from the right atrium to the right ventricle. From there, it is pumped to the lungs, where it exchanges carbon dioxide for oxygen.

- Blood flows from the lungs to the left atrium. From there, it flows to the left ventricle and is pumped through the aorta to the rest of the body.

- The brain and the **pacemaker** regulate how often the heart beats.

Blood Vessels

Key Concept: **The three main types of blood vessels are arteries, capillaries, and veins.**

- **Arteries** carry blood away from the heart. Most arteries, except those that carry blood from the heart to the lungs, carry oxygen-rich blood.

- **Capillaries** are the smallest blood vessels. Capillaries bring oxygen and nutrients to the cells, and take wastes from the cells.

- **Veins** are large, thin-walled blood vessels that carry blood to the heart.

- **Blood pressure** is the force with which blood pushes against vessels.

- Normal blood pressure is within the range of 90/60 to 119/79.

- **Hypertension** is blood pressure that is consistently 140/90 or higher.

Blood

Key Concept: **The four components of blood are plasma, red blood cells, white blood cells, and platelets.**

- **Plasma** is the liquid part of blood.

- **Red blood cells** carry oxygen from the lungs to all parts of the body.

- **White blood cells** help protect the body against disease.

- **Platelets** are cell fragments that help your blood clot.

- The four blood types are A, B, AB, and O.

Name _____ Class _____ Date _____

Note Taking Guide

Your Cardiovascular System (pp. 292–298)

Functions of the Cardiovascular System

1. What are the three main functions of the cardiovascular system?

   a. <u>delivering materials to cells</u>

   b. _____

   c. _____

The Heart

2. Complete the graphic organizer to trace the path of a blood cell, starting in the right atrium.

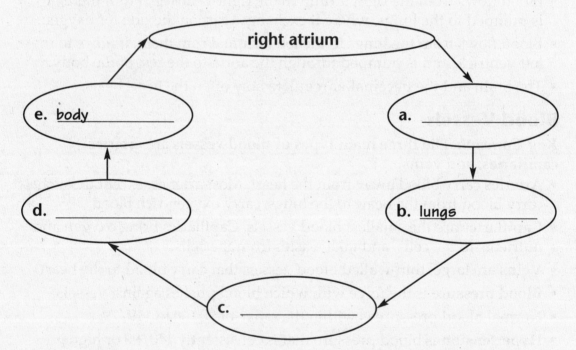

3. Fill in the blanks to complete the sentences that describe how the heart beats.

   First the **a.** _____ contract, pumping blood to the

   b. _____. Then the **c.** _____

   contract, pumping blood to the **d.** _____ and the rest of the body.

Section 12-1: **Note Taking Guide** (continued)

Blood Vessels

4. Complete the graphic organizer about blood vessels. Use the phrases from the box below.

smallest blood vessels	have thick, strong walls	carry blood to the heart
contain valves	deliver oxygen to cells	

Main Idea: The three main types of blood vessels in your body are arteries, capillaries, and veins.

Arteries

a. Function _carry blood away from the heart_

b. Structure _____

_____

_____

_____

Capillaries

c. Function _____

_____

_____

d. Structure _____

_____

_____

_____

Veins

e. Function _____

_____

_____

f. Structure _____

_____

_____

_____

5. Name the two readings in a blood pressure measurement and explain what each reading measures.

   a. The first reading is the _____.

   It is a measurement of blood pressure when the heart's ventricles

   _____.

   b. The second reading is the _____.

   It is a measurement of blood pressure when the heart's ventricles

   _____.

Name _____ Class _____ Date _____

Section 12-1: Note Taking Guide (continued)

Blood

6. Complete the table about the blood components. Use the terms from the box below.

| Platelets | Red blood cells | Plasma | White blood cells |

Blood Component	Description	Function
a. _____	straw-colored liquid made mostly of water	carries dissolved substances to cells and wastes to kidneys
b. _____	contain hemoglobin	carry oxygen from the lungs to all parts of the body
c. _____	larger but less numerous than red blood cells	help the body resist diseases
d. _____	cell fragments	release proteins to help blood to clot

7. Complete the table with the type of blood each patient could receive in a blood transfusion.

Patient	Can Receive Blood Type(s)
Patient 1: Type A	a. A and O
Patient 2: Type B	b. _____
Patient 3: Type AB	c. _____
Patient 4: Type O	d. _____

Name _____ Class _____ Date _____

Summary

Cardiovascular Health (pp. 299–303)

Cardiovascular Diseases

Key Concept: **Hypertension and high blood cholesterol are two factors that increase your risk of heart attack and stroke. Both factors may begin in your teens.**

- Hypertension is blood pressure that is consistently 140/90 or greater. Hypertension damages blood vessel walls and causes the heart muscle to work harder to pump blood through the body.

- Cholesterol is a component of cells, hormones, and nerve tissue. Cholesterol is transported in the blood by carriers called lipoproteins.

- **Low-density lipoproteins** (LDL) carry cholesterol to body tissues for use or storage. LDL is known as "bad cholesterol" because it can become a component of plaque.

- **Plaque** is a substance that builds up in artery walls.

- **Atherosclerosis** (ath uh roh skluh ROH sis) is a condition in which artery walls harden and thicken due to plaque buildup.

- **High-density lipoproteins** (HDL), or "good cholesterol," pick up excess cholesterol from tissues or artery walls and carry it to the liver, where it is excreted in bile.

- Atherosclerosis can lead to a heart attack or stroke.

- A heart murmur, an opening in the heart wall, or an arrhythmia can prevent the heart from functioning properly.

- An **arrhythmia** is an irregular heartbeat.

Keeping Healthy

Key Concept: **To help maintain cardiovascular health, you should exercise regularly; eat a nutrient-rich, balanced diet; and avoid smoking.**

- Teens should do 60 minutes of physical activity each day.

- To reduce your risk of cardiovascular disease, limit your intake of fried or processed foods and of foods made from animal products. Eating high-fiber foods may help keep your blood cholesterol levels low.

- Tobacco products damage blood vessels and contribute to the development of atherosclerosis and hypertension.

Section 12-2 *Note Taking Guide*

Cardiovascular Health (pp. 299–303)

Cardiovascular Diseases

1. Complete the outline by adding important details about cardiovascular diseases.

I. Cardiovascular Diseases

   A. Hypertension

      1. Description <u>blood pressure consistently 140/90 or greater</u>

      2. Effect <u>damages blood vessel walls; causes heart to pump harder</u>

   B. Blood cholesterol

      1. Low-density lipoprotein

         a. Description _____

         b. Effect _____

      2. High-density lipoprotein

         a. Description _____

         b. Effect _____

   C. Heart attack and stroke

      1. Heart attack

      Description _____

      2. Stroke

      Description _____

   D. Other cardiovascular diseases

      1. Heart murmur

      Description _____

      2. Opening in heart wall

      Description _____

      3. Arrhythmia

      Description _____

Name _____ Class _____ Date _____

Section 12-2: **Note Taking Guide** *(continued)*

Keeping Healthy

2. Complete the concept map about risk factors for cardiovascular disease. Use the words and phrases from the box below.

family history	diet	not smoking

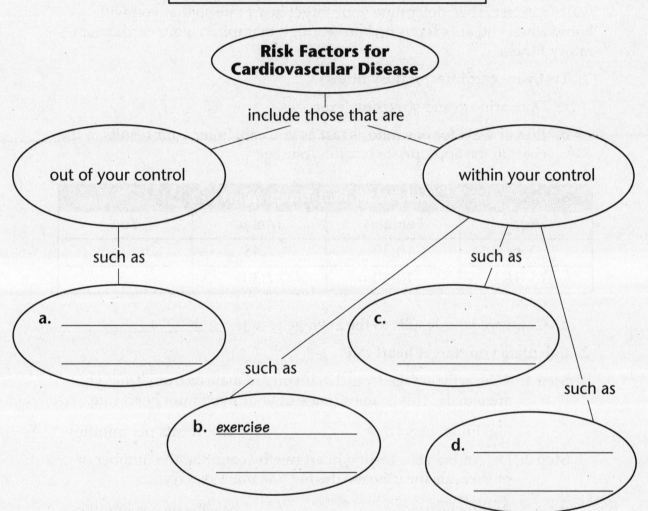

Chapter 12 | *Building Health Skills*

Improving Your Cardiorespiratory Fitness
(pp. 304–305)

Measure your cardiorespiratory fitness by performing a one-mile walk/run test. Then determine your target heart rate so that you will know when you are exercising hard enough to improve your cardiorespiratory fitness.

1. Test your cardiorespiratory fitness.

    a. Do warm-up and stretching exercises.

    b. Run or walk for one mile as fast as you can. Enter your results in the chart in the appropriate box for your age.

Mile Walk/Run Times (min)			
Age	**Females**	**Males**	**You**
14	10:30	7:45	
15–18	10:30	7:30	

    c. Compare your results to the average results. _____

2. Calculate your target heart rate.

    Step 1: Subtract your age from 220 if you are male or from 226 if you are female. This is an estimate of your maximum heart rate.

        Maximum heart rate: _____ heartbeats per minute.

    Step 2: Determine your resting heart rate by counting the number of pulse beats (heartbeats) during one minute at rest.

        Resting heart rate: _____ heartbeats per minute.

    Step 3: Subtract your resting heart rate from your maximum heart rate.

        _____ – _____ = _____

        (maximum heart rate) (resting heart rate)

    Step 4: Multiply the number from Step 3 above by 0.6 and round to the nearest whole number. Then multiply the number from Step 3 above by 0.8 and round to the nearest whole number.

        _____ × 0.6 = _____

        _____ × 0.8 = _____

Improving Your Cardiorespiratory Fitness (continued)

Step 5: Add your resting heart rate to each of the two numbers you obtained in Step 4 to find your target heart rate range.

_____ + _____ = _____ heartbeats per minute
(resting   (from Step 4)
heart rate)

_____ + _____ = _____ heartbeats per minute
(resting   (from Step 4)
heart rate)

3. **Choose an exercise program.**

   a. List activities you can do to improve your cardiorespiratory fitness.

   _____

   b. After several weeks, repeat the walk/run fitness test to check your progress. Did your results change? _____

   _____

Name _____ Class _____ Date _____

Summary

Respiratory Health (pp. 306–310)

The Respiratory System

Key Concept: **The respiratory system is responsible for bringing oxygen from the outside environment into the body. It also removes carbon dioxide from the body.**

• Blood carries oxygen from the lungs to body cells. After cells use oxygen to break down glucose, they are left with carbon dioxide. Blood carries carbon dioxide to the lungs to be removed from the body.

Key Concept: **On its way to the lungs, air passes through the nose, pharynx, larynx, trachea, and bronchi.**

• At the ends of the smallest tubes in the lungs are tiny sacs called **alveoli** (al VEE uh ly). Gases are exchanged between the air and the blood at the alveoli.

Key Concept: **The breathing process is controlled by the actions of muscles in your ribs and chest.**

• The **diaphragm** (DY uh fram) is a dome-shaped muscle that lies below the lungs. When you inhale, or breathe in, the diaphragm flattens, and the chest cavity expands to allow air to flow into the lungs.

• When you exhale, or breathe out, the diaphragm moves upward. The rib muscles relax and the ribs drop. These movements make the chest cavity smaller and force air out of the lungs.

Keeping Healthy

Key Concept: **You can keep your respiratory system healthy by avoiding tobacco smoke and air pollution and treating asthma if you have it. In addition, avoid respiratory infections, get regular exercise, and maintain a healthy weight.**

• The most important thing you can do to protect your respiratory system is not to smoke. It is also important to avoid exposure to air pollutants whenever possible.

• **Asthma** (AZ muh) is a disorder in which respiratory passageways become inflamed. During an asthma attack, the passageways narrow until air can barely pass through, causing breathing difficulty.

• **Bronchitis** is an infection that causes the mucous membranes lining the bronchi to become inflamed. The inflamed membranes secrete mucus that must be removed by coughing.

Section 12-3

Note Taking Guide

Respiratory Health (pp. 306–310)

The Respiratory System

1. Complete the flowchart about the pathway that air takes into your body. Use the words from the box below.

trachea	larynx
lungs	bronchi
pharynx	

a. _nose_ _____

↓

b. _____

↓

c. _____

↓

d. _____

↓

e. _____

↓

f. _____

Section 12-3: **Note Taking Guide** *(continued)*

2. Complete the table about the breathing process. Use the words and phrases from the box below.

| pull ribs up and out | relax and ribs drop | enlarges |
| gets smaller | flattens | moves upward |

Stage	Action
Inhalation	**a.** rib muscles _____; **b.** the diaphragm _____; **c.** the chest cavity _____
Exhalation	**d.** rib muscles _____; **e.** the diaphragm _____; **f.** the chest cavity _____

Keeping Healthy

3. Explain why each of the following behaviors can help keep your respiratory system healthy.

a. Avoid smoking <u>Exposure to smoke damages the respiratory system.</u>

_____

b. Avoid air pollution _____

_____

c. Treat asthma if you have it _____

_____

d. Avoid respiratory infections _____

_____

e. Get regular exercise _____

_____

f. Maintain a healthy weight _____

_____

Section 13-1 *Summary*

The Importance of Physical Activity (pp. 316–321)

The Benefits of Physical Activity

Key Concept: The changes that occur due to physical activity are beneficial to your body, your mind, and your social interactions.

- Any movement that requires your large muscle groups to work is considered **physical activity.**
- Exercise benefits your heart, blood vessels, and bones; helps you maintain a healthy weight; and improves balance and coordination.
- During continuous exercise, your brain releases **endorphins,** chemicals that block pain messages from reaching your brain cells.

The Components of Fitness

Key Concept: There are five components of fitness: cardiorespiratory endurance, muscular strength, muscular endurance, flexibility, and body composition.

- **Physical fitness** means that you have the energy and strength to participate in a variety of activities.
- Cardiorespiratory endurance means heart and lungs work efficiently.
- Muscular strength is the ability of your muscles to produce force. Muscular endurance is the ability of muscles to work over time.
- Flexibility is the ability to move a joint through its range of motions.
- **Body composition** is the amount of fat tissue in your body compared to the amount of lean tissue, such as muscles and bones.

Types of Physical Activity

Key Concept: Physical activities can be classified as aerobic exercise or anaerobic exercise. Strengthening and endurance activities can be further classified as isometric exercise, isotonic exercise, and isokinetic exercise.

- Ongoing physical activity that raises your breathing rate and heart rate is called **aerobic exercise** (ehr OH bik).
- Intense physical activity that lasts for a few seconds to a few minutes is called **anaerobic exercise** (an uh ROH bik).
- An **isometric exercise** (eye suh MET rik) is an exercise in which muscles contract but very little body movement takes place.
- **Isotonic exercise** (eye suh TAHN ik) involves contracting and relaxing a muscle through the full range of a joint's motion.
- In **isokinetic exercise** (eye soh ki NET ik) muscles contract at a constant rate with use of a special exercise machine.

Name _____ Class _____ Date _____

Note Taking Guide

The Importance of Physical Activity (pp. 316–321)

The Benefits of Physical Activity

1. Complete the graphic organizer about the benefits of physical activity. Use the phrases from the box below.

stronger bones	reduced stress level	bonding with family and friends
increased self-confidence	maintaining weight	building new relationships
having fun	improved mood	healthier cardiovascular system

Main Idea: Physical activity is beneficial to your body, your mind, and your social interactions.

Physical Benefits

a. _____

b. _____

c. _____

Psychological Benefits

d. _____

e. _____

f. _____

Social Benefits

g. _____

h. _____

i. _____

The Components of Fitness

2. Briefly describe the five components of fitness.

a. _____

b. _____

c. _____

d. _____

e. _____

Name _____ Class _____ Date _____

Section 13-1: **Note Taking Guide** (continued)

Types of Physical Activity

3. Complete the table about types of physical activity. Use the words from the box below.

| Aerobic | Isokinetic | Isotonic | Isometric | Anaerobic |

Type of Exercise	Description	Examples
a. _____	ongoing physical activity that raises your breathing rate and heart rate	swimming, running, brisk walking, cross-country skiing
b. _____	intense physical activity that lasts from a few seconds to a few minutes	lifting weights, doing push-ups, sprinting
c. _____	muscles contract but very little body movement takes place	placing palms together and pushing them against each other
d. _____	contracting and relaxing muscles through the full range of a joint's motion	exercising with free weights such as barbells
e. _____	muscles contract at a constant rate	using a fitness machine that provides resistance to muscle movement

Name _____ Class _____ Date _____

Chapter 13 | Building Health Skills

Assessing Flexibility, Muscular Strength, and Endurance (pp. 322–323)

It is important to know your current level of fitness before planning a fitness program. Use this worksheet to measure your flexibility, muscular strength, and endurance.

1. **Assess your flexibility.**

   Perform this test four times. Record the distance your fingers reached on the fourth trial in the appropriate box below.

Flexibility Fitness Level			
Age	Males	Females	You
13	+0.5 in.	+3.5 in.	
14	+1.0 in.	+4.5 in.	
15	+2.0 in.	+5.0 in.	
16–17	+3.0 in.	+5.5 in.	

2. **Assess your abdominal muscular strength and endurance.**

   Have your partner count aloud the number of curl-ups you complete in one minute. Record your result in the chart below.

Curl-ups Fitness Level			
Age	Males	Females	You
13–17	45/min	37/min	

STOP

© Pearson Education, Inc., publishing as Pearson Prentice Hall. All rights reserved.

152-A

Name _____ Class _____ Date _____

Assessing Flexibility, Muscular Strength, and Endurance *(continued)*

3. Assess your upper body muscular strength and endurance.

Continue doing push-ups until you cannot complete one every three seconds. Record your result in the appropriate box below.

Push-ups Fitness Level			
Age	**Males**	**Females**	**You**
13–14	24	11	
15–16	30	15	
17	37	16	

4. How did your performance on the three fitness tests compare with the average fitness level shown for your age and gender?

_____

_____

_____

_____

5. Do you feel you need to improve in one or more of these areas of fitness? If so, write your plan to improve each area in the space below.

_____

_____

_____

_____

_____

_____

Section 13-2 *Summary*

Setting Goals for Lifelong Fitness (pp. 324–329)

Planning a Fitness Program

Key Concept: **To plan a successful fitness program you should define your goals, develop your program, and monitor your progress.**

- If you get into the habit of exercising now, it will help you maintain **lifelong fitness**—the ability to stay healthy and fit as you age.
- The success of your fitness plan depends, in part, on the **FITT formula,** which stands for frequency, intensity, time, and type.
- Your **target heart rate** is the rate at which your cardiovascular system receives the most benefits from exercise without working too hard.
- To prevent boredom and overuse injuries, you should practice **cross-training** by participating in a wide variety of activities.

Phases of Exercise

Key Concept: **The safest workouts begin with a warm-up period and end with a cool-down period. Stretching exercises should be part of both the warm-up and cool-down periods.**

- A warm-up is a five- to ten-minute period of mild exercise that prepares your body for a vigorous workout.
- When you stretch, you should feel tension, but not pain.
- The workout is when you perform an activity at its peak level.
- The cool-down is a period of mild exercise, such as walking, performed after a workout.
- Stretching after your cool-down loosens muscles that may have tightened during exercise.

Section 13-2 *Note Taking Guide*

Setting Goals for Lifelong Fitness (pp. 324–329)

Planning a Fitness Program

1. Complete the outline about planning a fitness program. Use the phrases from the box below.

Define short-term goals	Develop your fitness plan	The FITT formula
Alter your fitness plan	Define long-term goals	Monitor your progress

   I. Planning a Fitness Program

   A. _____

       1. Choose activities that you enjoy.

       2. Vary your activities from day to day.

       3. Combine exercise with social activities.

   B. _____

       1. Make your goals specific.

       2. Make your time frame realistic.

   C. _____

       1. Mark a calendar with a weekly exercise plan.

       2. Consider health concerns.

       3. Consider your budget.

       4. Consider where you live.

   D. _____

       1. Frequency   3. Time

       2. Intensity   4. Type

   E. _____

       1. Track overall progress using a chart.

       2. Monitor your resting heart rate.

   F. _____

       1. Slightly increase time or intensity of workouts.

       2. Combine exercise with healthy eating habits.

Section 13-2: **Note Taking Guide** (continued)

Phases of Exercise

2. Complete the flowchart about the phases of exercise. Use the words or phrases from the box below.

Cardiorespiratory workout	Warm-up	Stretch
Strength/endurance workout	Stretch	Cool-down

Phases of Exercise

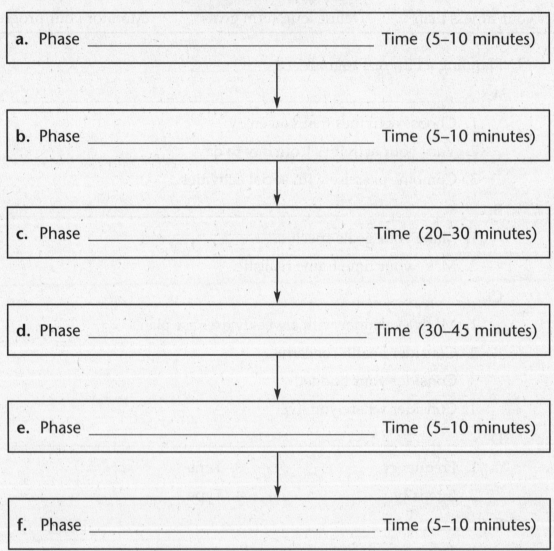

a. Phase _____ Time (5–10 minutes)

b. Phase _____ Time (5–10 minutes)

c. Phase _____ Time (20–30 minutes)

d. Phase _____ Time (30–45 minutes)

e. Phase _____ Time (5–10 minutes)

f. Phase _____ Time (5–10 minutes)

Section 13-3 *Summary*

Physical Activity and Safety (pp. 331–336)

Exercising Safely

Key Concept: Most injuries can be avoided if you get proper medical care, wear safety equipment, and pay attention to your surroundings and the weather. Proper water and food intake is also important.

- A safe fitness plan starts with a visit to your doctor.
- A key to exercising safely is to choose the right equipment for your particular activity.
- In planning your exercise program take into account where you live and where it is safe to exercise.
- Make sure your clothing is appropriate for the weather.
- Replacing the water you lose in sweat will prevent **dehydration,** or excessive water loss.

Avoiding Harmful Substances

Key Concept: To achieve and maintain lifelong fitness, you need to avoid substances that can harm you.

- A **dietary supplement** is any product that contains one or more vitamins, minerals, herbs, or other dietary substances that may be lacking in the diet. Although some people benefit from supplements, healthy teens should try to get their nutrients from a proper diet.
- Anabolic steroids are artificial forms of the hormone testosterone, a hormone that is involved in muscle development.
- People who take steroids for non-medical reasons are putting both their short- and long-term health at risk.

Preventing Sports-Related Injuries

Key Concept: An important part of achieving lifelong fitness is avoiding overtraining and preventing injuries.

- If you exercise too intensely or for too long without allowing enough time for rest, you may be **overtraining.**
- You can avoid overtraining by sticking to a consistent exercise schedule that includes days of rest.
- Using the same joints repetitively during workouts can lead to overuse injuries.
- Allowing sports-related injuries to heal properly is very important for lifelong fitness.

Section 13-3 Note Taking Guide

Physical Activity and Safety (pp. 331–336)

Exercising Safely

1. Complete the concept map about exercising safely. Use the terms and phrases from the box below.

footwear	proper food and water intake	awareness of surroundings
protective gear	attention to weather	safety equipment

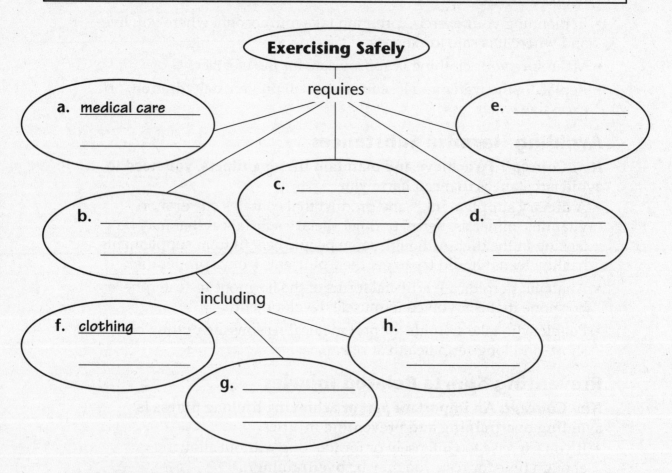

Avoiding Harmful Substances

2. What precautions should you keep in mind about dietary supplements?

_____ a. They may make you too healthy.

_____ b. They do not undergo the same strict testing as medications do.

_____ c. There is no guarantee that they will provide all the benefits that they claim.

Section 13-3: **Note Taking Guide** (continued)

3. Compare the effects of steroids on the male body and the female body by completing the Venn diagram. Write similarities where the circles overlap, and differences on the left and right sides.

liver problems	stunted growth	facial hair growth	hair loss
mood swings	infertility	liver and kidney cancer	acne
enlarged breasts	cardiovascular disease	deepening of voice	

Effects of Steroids on the Body

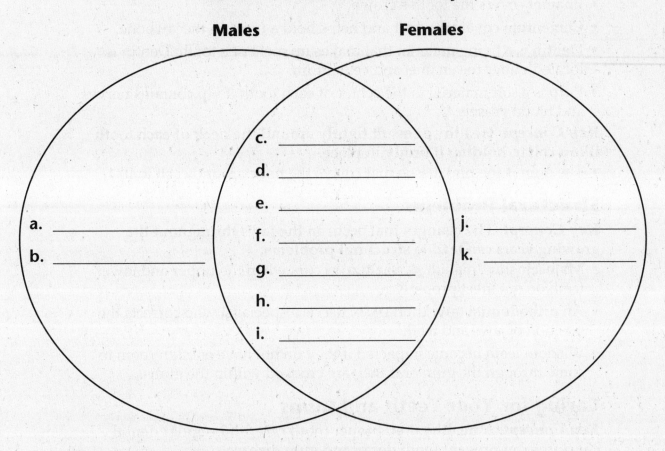

Males   **Females**

a. _____

b. _____

c. _____

d. _____

e. _____

f. _____

g. _____

h. _____

i. _____

j. _____

k. _____

Preventing Sports-Related Injuries

4. List the signs of overtraining.

<u>fatigue during exercise or a few hours later</u>

_____

5. What common injuries can usually be treated using the R.I.C.E. method?

a. _____

b. _____

Name _____ Class _____ Date _____

Summary

Your Teeth and Gums (pp. 342–346)

The Teeth and Gums

Key Concept: **Healthy teeth allow you to chew your food properly and speak clearly.**

- You have four kinds of teeth: incisors, canines, premolars, and molars. The basic parts of a tooth are the crown, the neck, and the root.
- **Enamel** covers the tooth's crown.
- **Cementum** covers the root and helps hold a tooth in the jawbone.
- **Dentin** is a living material that makes up most of a tooth. Dentin is located under the enamel and cementum.
- **Pulp** is a soft material in the center of each tooth. Pulp contains nerves and blood vessels.

Key Concept: **Healthy gums fit tightly around the neck of each tooth like a collar, holding it firmly in place.**

- The gum is the pink tissue that covers the bone around each tooth.

Structural Problems

Key Concept: **The changes that occur in the jaws throughout the growing years can lead to structural problems.**

- **Malocclusion** (mal uh KLOO zhun) occurs when the upper and lower teeth do not meet properly.
- An **orthodontist** (awr thuh DAHN tist) is a specialist who corrects the position of jaws and teeth.
- Wisdom teeth become impacted if they do not have enough room to come through the gum or if they are crooked within the gums.

Caring for Your Teeth and Gums

Key Concept: **A healthy diet, proper tooth care, and regular dental checkups can prevent tooth decay and gum disease.**

- Not taking care of teeth can lead to pain and **halitosis,** or bad breath.
- A diet that is low in sugar will help keep bacteria in your mouth from producing an acid that can damage your teeth.
- **Plaque** is a film that sticks to your teeth. Brushing and flossing removes food and plaque from teeth and in between teeth.
- A mouthguard prevents damage to teeth during contact sports.
- Regular dental checkups can identify tooth problems early.
- Plaque that is not removed from teeth hardens into a material called **tartar.** If not removed, plaque and tartar can lead to **periodontal disease,** or gum disease. Gingivitis is the early stage of gum disease.

Section 14-1 Note Taking Guide

Your Teeth and Gums (pp. 342–346)

The Teeth and Gums

1. List the four types of teeth found in your mouth.

    a. <u>incisors</u>   c. _____

    b. _____   d. _____

2. List and describe the three types of bonelike material found in each tooth.

    a. <u>Enamel: the hardest material in your body; covers a tooth's crown</u>

    b. _____

    c. _____

Structural Problems

3. Complete the table about structural problems of the jaws or teeth.

Structural Problem	Description	Effects
a. _____ _____	when the upper and lower teeth do not meet properly; an improper bite	b. _____ _____ c. _____ _____
d. _____ _____	teeth may not have the space to emerge through the gum line; teeth may be positioned at an awkward angle	e. _____ _____

Section 14-1: **Note Taking Guide** (continued)

Caring for Your Teeth and Gums

4. Complete the table about caring for your teeth and gums.

Action	Benefit
a. Healthy diet	prevents bacteria from producing acids that can damage your teeth
b. _____	removes plaque and food particles from teeth
c. _____	removes food and plaque from areas that a toothbrush cannot reach

5. List two types of preventive care that have reduced the number of cavities in young people.

    a. regular dentist visits _____

    b. _____

    _____

6. Describe the two stages of periodontal disease.

    a. gingivitis: gums become red and swollen and bleed easily _____

    b. _____

    _____

    _____

Section 14-2 *Summary*

Your Skin, Hair, and Nails (pp. 347–353)

Your Skin

Key Concept: **The skin covers and protects the body from injury, infection, and water loss. The skin also helps to control body temperature and gathers information from the environment.**

- Sweat glands and blood vessels in skin help regulate body temperature.
- Nerves supply information about pressure, pain, and temperature.
- The **epidermis** (ep uh DUR mis) is the outmost layer of skin. The protein **keratin** makes the skin tough and waterproof. **Melanin** is a dark pigment that gives skin some of its color.
- The **dermis** (DUR mis) is the layer of skin under the epidermis. Sweat, produced in glands in the dermis, comes to the surface through openings called **pores.** Hair grows from **follicles.** Oil that keeps hair and skin soft and moist is released by **sebaceous glands.**

Caring for Your Skin

Key Concept: **The most important things you can do for your skin are to avoid damage from the sun and tanning lamps and to monitor moles.**

- Basic skin care includes regular washing with soap, eating a healthy diet, drinking plenty of water, and getting enough sleep.
- Sun damage can lead to **melanoma,** a deadly form of cancer. The first sign of melanoma is often an irregularly shaped mole.
- **Acne** forms when oil and dead cells plug a hair follicle.
- A **dermatologist** is a doctor who specializes in treating skin problems.
- Skin problems include **eczema** (EK suh muh), a condition in which skin becomes red, swollen, hot, and itchy.

Your Hair

Key Concept: **Hair protects the scalp from sunlight and provides insulation from the cold. Hairs in the nostrils and ears and your eyelashes prevent debris from entering the body.**

- Hair problems include head lice and dandruff.

Your Nails

Key Concept: **Tough, platelike nails cover and protect the tips of your fingers and toes.**

- Keep nails clean and smooth to stop the spread of microorganisms.
- Ingrown toenails happen when the sides of a nail grow into the skin.

Name _____ Class _____ Date _____

Note Taking Guide

Your Skin, Hair, and Nails (pp. 347–353)

Your Skin

1. Complete the graphic organizer about the functions of your skin. Use the terms from the box below.

Information Gathering	Protection	Temperature Regulation

Main Idea: The skin covers and protects the body from injury, infection, and water loss. The skin also helps to regulate body temperature and gathers information from the environment.

a. _____
_____

b. _____
_____

c. _____
_____

shields and protects organs and tissues; keeps harmful substances out; keeps important fluids in

helps cool body; blood vessels widen to release heat; blood vessels become narrow to keep heat in

nerves provide information to your central nervous system about pressure, pain, and temperature

2. Describe the two major layers of skin.

a. _____

_____

b. _____

_____

Section 14-2: Note Taking Guide (continued)

Caring for Your Skin

3. Complete the table with details about skin problems.

Skin Problems	Description and Cause	Prevention
a. skin damage _____ _____	Skin becomes wrinkled, leathery, and discolored	b. _____ _____
c. _____ _____	Occurs when oil and dead skin cells clog follicles	d. _____ _____
e. _____ _____	Irritation of skin that makes it red, hot, and itchy	f. _____ _____
g. _____ _____	Caused by many types of microorganisms	h. _____ _____

Your Hair

4. List two hair care tips you should follow to keep your hair healthy.

   a. _____

   b. _____

Your Nails

5. List two nail care tips you should follow to keep your nails healthy.

   a. _____

   b. _____

Chapter 14 Building Health Skills

Recognizing Misleading Claims (pp. 354–355)

Each year millions of people spend billions of dollars on health products that promise perfect, blemish-free skin, rapid weight loss, or greater energy. However, not all the products really do what they claim. Many consumers find such ads convincing, and buy the products without thinking critically about their claims. By doing so, they may not only waste money but also risk their health.

How can you recognize misleading claims? Use this worksheet to help you analyze the claims made by a product.

1. **Examine the product's claims for misleading information.**

   List six questions you should ask yourself when evaluating a product.

   a. <u>Do any of the claims contradict common knowledge?</u>

   b. _____

   _____

   _____

   c. _____

   _____

   _____

   d. _____

   _____

   _____

   e. _____

   _____

   _____

   f. _____

   _____

   _____

Recognizing Misleading Claims (continued)

2. **Try to check any claims made about the product.**

   List two ways to check for claims made about the product before purchasing it.

   a. _____

   _____

   _____

   b. _____

   _____

   _____

3. **Request more information.**

   Where can you obtain more information about a product?

   a. _____

   _____

   _____

   b. _____

   _____

   _____

Section 14-3 **Summary**

Your Eyes and Ears (pp. 356–363)

Your Eyes

Key Concept: **The eyes are complex organs that respond to light by sending impulses. Your brain then interprets these impulses as images.**

- Light first strikes your **cornea** (KAWR nee uh), a clear tissue that covers the front of the eye.

- The **pupil** is the opening through which light enters the eye. The **iris**, the circular, colored structure around the pupil, controls the pupil's size.

- The **lens** is a flexible structure that focuses light.

- The **retina** is a layer of cells that lines the back of the eye. Rods and cones in the retina send impulses through the optic nerve to the brain.

Caring for Your Eyes

Key Concept: **It is important to protect your eyes from damage and to have regular eye exams.**

- Wear protective goggles around harmful materials and machinery. Wear sunglasses to protect eyes from UV light rays.

- An **optometrist** provides eye care and checks for vision problems.

- Nearsightedness, farsightedness, and astigmatism are common vision problems that can usually be fixed by eyeglasses or contact lenses.

Your Ears

Key Concept: **Your ears convert sounds into nerve impulses that your brain interprets. In addition, structures in the ear sense the position and movement of your head.**

- The outer ear sends vibrations to the **eardrum,** a thin membrane at the end of the ear canal. The eardrum transfers vibrations to the middle ear.

- The **cochlea** is a hollow, coiled, fluid-filled tube that forms the inner ear. When the fluid moves, tiny hairs cause messages to be sent to the brain.

- **Semicircular canals** are structures in the inner ear that send information to the brain about the movements of your head.

Caring for Your Ears

Key Concept: **Besides keeping your ears clean, you also need to monitor noise levels. See a doctor if you have ear pain or hearing difficulties.**

- Keeping televisions, stereos, and personal music players at reasonable volumes will help prevent hearing loss as you age.

- An **audiologist** is trained to detect and treat hearing loss.

Section 14-3 Note Taking Guide

Your Eyes and Ears (pp. 356–363)

Your Eyes

1. Complete the table by identifying the structure in your eyes. Use the words from the box below.

| Iris | Pupil | Retina | Lens | Cornea |

Structure	Description
a. _____	the clear tissue that covers the front of the eye
b. _____	the opening through which light enters the eye
c. _____	circular structure that surrounds the pupil and controls its size
d. _____	flexible structure that focuses light
e. _____	a layer of cells that lines the back of the eye

Caring for Your Eyes

2. Complete the graphic organizer by identifying the cause and effect of each vision problem.

Vision Problem	Cause	Effect
Nearsightedness	a. *an elongated eyeball*	b. *trouble seeing faraway objects*
Farsightedness	c. _____	d. _____
Astigmatism	e. _____	f. _____

Section 14-3: Note Taking Guide (continued)

3. Complete the concept map with causes of eye problems.

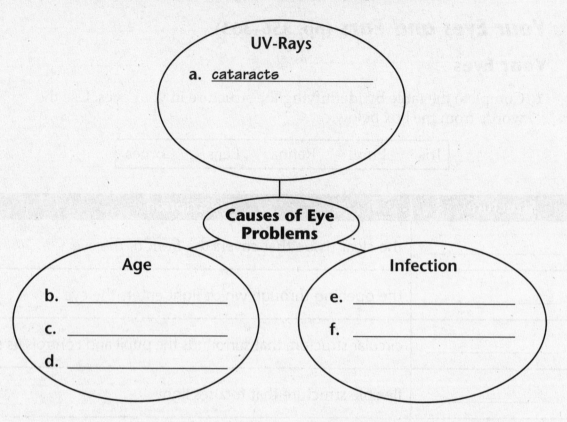

UV-Rays

a. <u>cataracts</u>

Causes of Eye Problems

Age

b. _____

c. _____

d. _____

Infection

e. _____

f. _____

4. Put a check mark next to the eye care tips you can follow to reduce eyestrain.

_____ **a.** Blink often when using a computer.

_____ **b.** Rub your eyes.

_____ **c.** Look away from a computer every 30 minutes.

5. How can you help protect your eyes from the sun?

_____

_____

Section 14-3: **Note Taking Guide** (continued)

Your Ears

6. Complete the flowchart with details about how sound waves travel through the ear.

```
┌─────────────────────────────────────────────────────────────┐
│                         Outer Ear                            │
│                                                              │
│  a.  Sound travels through the ear canal and strikes the     │
│      eardrum.                                                 │
│      _____     │
└─────────────────────────────────────────────────────────────┘
                              │
                              ▼
┌─────────────────────────────────────────────────────────────┐
│                        Middle Ear                            │
│                                                              │
│  b.  _____     │
│      _____     │
└─────────────────────────────────────────────────────────────┘
                              │
                              ▼
┌─────────────────────────────────────────────────────────────┐
│                        Inner Ear                             │
│                                                              │
│  c.  _____     │
│      _____     │
└─────────────────────────────────────────────────────────────┘
                              │
                              ▼
┌─────────────────────────────────────────────────────────────┐
│                           Brain                              │
│                                                              │
│  d.  _____     │
│      _____     │
└─────────────────────────────────────────────────────────────┘
```

Caring for Your Ears

7. List two things you can do to care for your ears.

a. _____

b. _____

Section 14-4 **Summary**

Sleep and Feeling Fit (pp. 364–366)

What Is Sleep?

Key Concept: **Although some people think of sleep as wasted time, it is actually as important to the body as air, water, and food.**

- Sleep is the deep relaxation of the body and mind during which the eyes are usually closed and there is little conscious thought or movement.
- Sleep helps learning and memory, healing, the immune system, and may help prevent diseases.
- The sleep cycle consists of nonrapid eye movement sleep (NREM) followed by rapid eye movement sleep (REM).
- Dreaming takes place during REM sleep. About one quarter of your sleeping time is REM sleep.
- Sleep disorders can affect health and should be treated by a doctor.
- A person with **insomnia** has trouble falling asleep or staying asleep.
- **Sleep apnea** is a disorder in which a person stops breathing during sleep for short periods and then starts breathing again.
- **Narcolepsy** is a disorder in which a person is very sleepy during the day or falls asleep suddenly.

Teens and Sleep

Key Concept: **Puberty affects the body's circadian rhythm. One result is that teens want to sleep later into the day and stay awake later at night than adults.**

- The sleep cycle is controlled by the body's **circadian rhythm,** which is the body's internal system for regulating behavior patterns in a 24-hour cycle.
- Most teens need about nine hours of sleep each night.
- Teens sleep an average of seven hours a night. Depression, trouble paying attention, and increased risk of illness and motor-vehicle crashes are some of the effects of sleep loss.

Section 14-4 **Note Taking Guide**

Sleep and Feeling Fit (pp. 364–366)

What Is Sleep?

1. List four benefits of sleep.

   a. <u>learning and memory storage take place</u>

   b. _____

   c. _____

   d. _____

2. Complete the table about sleep disorders. Use the words from the box below.

   | Sleep apnea | Narcolepsy | Insomnia |

Sleep Disorder	Description
a. _____	difficulty falling asleep or staying asleep
b. _____	a disorder that causes you to stop breathing for short periods of time during sleep and then suddenly start breathing again
c. _____	a disorder that causes you to feel extremely sleepy during the day or to fall asleep suddenly

Teens and Sleep

3. List four tips that can help you develop good sleep habits.

   a. <u>Go to bed and wake up at the same times each day, even on weekends.</u>

   b. _____

   c. _____

   d. _____

Name _____ Class _____ Date _____

Summary

Alcohol Is a Drug (pp. 374–377)

Facts About Alcohol

Key Concept: **Alcohol slows the body's normal reactions. Alcohol may cause confusion, decreased alertness, poor coordination, blurred vision, and drowsiness.**

• A **drug** is a chemical substance that is taken to cause changes in a person's body or behavior. Alcohol is a drug.

• A **depressant** (dih PRES unt) is a drug that slows brain and body reactions. Alcohol is a depressant.

• Alcohol is produced by a process called **fermentation.** During fermentation, microorganisms called yeast feed on the sugars in certain foods. The result is that carbon dioxide and alcohol are produced.

• The alcohol content of alcoholic beverages varies. It typically ranges from 4 percent to 50 percent.

Teens and Alcohol

Key Concept: **The attitudes of peers, family, and the media strongly influence underage drinking.**

• Alcohol is illegal for people under the age of 21.

• Under a **zero-tolerance policy** practiced by many schools, students face consequences the first time they are caught with alcohol or other drugs on school grounds.

• Other teens, parents, and family members influence teens' decisions about alcohol.

• Advertisements for alcohol give the false impression that drinking makes young people more popular and attractive.

• Teens who use alcohol are more likely to be injured or killed in a motor vehicle crash, and are more likely to be a victim of sexual assault or violence. Underage drinkers also face legal risks, such as seizure of property, fines, loss of driver's license, or jail time.

Section 15-1 Note Taking Guide

Alcohol Is a Drug (pp. 374–377)

Facts About Alcohol

1. Put a check mark next to three depressant effects of alcohol.

_____ **a.** confusion   _____ **d.** drowsiness

_____ **b.** fermentation   _____ **e.** poor coordination

_____ **c.** weight loss

Teens and Alcohol

2. Complete the concept map about the use of alcohol. Use the terms from the box below.

> legal problems   injury and death   media
> family   peers

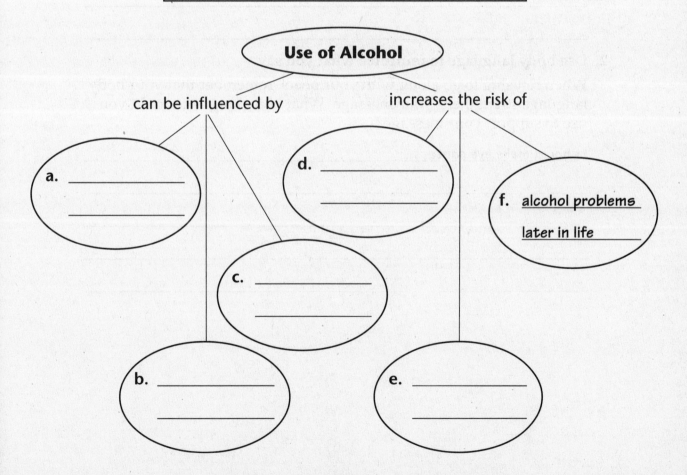

Name _____ Class _____ Date _____

Chapter 15

Building Health Skills

Developing Refusal Skills (pp. 378–379)

Imagine that your peers are trying to pressure you to do something you do not want to do. What refusal skills would you use? Use this worksheet to practice the ways you can resist peer pressure. Practice how to say *no* convincingly.

Imagine a situation in which your peers are pressuring you. They want you to drink alcohol with them. You do not want to participate. You use your refusal skills.

1. **Give a reason for your refusal.**

   Think of at least two honest reasons that you could give your peers for refusing alcohol. Write them below.

   <u>I'm not old enough to drink.</u>_____

   _____

   _____

   _____

2. **Use body language to reinforce what you say.**

   When refusing to go along with your peers, remember that your body language strengthens your message. What body language could you use to support your message?

   <u>I should make eye contact.</u>_____

   _____

   _____

   _____

Developing Refusal Skills (continued)

3. Show your concern for others.

How can you express your concern for those who are trying to persuade you? Write at least two things you could say.

What if you do something you regret? _____

_____

_____

4. Provide alternatives.

Are there activities that you can suggest to your peers that would be safer and more comfortable? List at least two.

Let's go bowling instead. _____

_____

_____

_____

5. Take a definite action.

What if your peers still try to persuade you after you have made your feelings clear? List some specific actions that you could take to leave the situation.

I could call a family member. _____

_____

_____

_____

Section 15-2 **Summary**

Alcohol's Effects on the Body (pp. 380–385)

Physical and Behavioral Effects

Key Concept: **Many negative effects on a drinker's body and behavior occur with intoxication by alcohol.**

- Alcohol is absorbed into the blood from the stomach. Then it circulates throughout the body.
- **Intoxication** is the state in which a person's mental and physical abilities are impaired by alcohol or another substance.
- Intoxication affects the nervous system, the cardiovascular system, the digestive system, and the excretory system.
- Intoxication may lead to loss of judgment and self-control, and blackouts.
- A **blackout** is a period of time that a drinker cannot recall. Blackouts can happen to first-time drinkers as well as to experienced drinkers.

Blood Alcohol Concentration

Key Concept: **The rate of alcohol consumption, the gender and size of the drinker, and how much food is in the stomach all affect BAC.**

- **Blood alcohol concentration (BAC)** is the amount of alcohol in the blood, expressed as a percentage.
- The higher a person's BAC, the more severe the physical and behavioral effects of alcohol.
- After a person stops drinking, BAC begins to decrease.
- A **hangover** is a term used to describe the aftereffects of drinking too much alcohol. Symptoms include nausea, upset stomach, headache, and sensitivity to noise.

Life-Threatening Effects

Key Concept: **Intoxication increases the risk of death from motor vehicle crashes, alcohol overdose, and interactions of alcohol with other drugs.**

- **Driving while intoxicated (DWI)** is a charge given to a driver whose BAC exceeds the legal limit.
- It is illegal for minors to drive after drinking any amount of alcohol.
- Taking an excessive amount of a drug that leads to coma or death is called an **overdose.**
- **Binge drinking**—drinking excessive amounts of alcohol at one time—can result in an overdose.
- Mixing alcohol with other drugs can be extremely dangerous or fatal.

Name _____ Class _____ Date _____

Note Taking Guide

Alcohol's Effects on the Body (pp. 380–385)

Physical and Behavioral Effects

1. Complete the concept map about the effects of intoxication on body systems and behavior. Use the terms and phrases from the box below.

digestive system	excretory system	loss of judgment and self-control
nervous system	decrease of natural fears	cardiovascular system

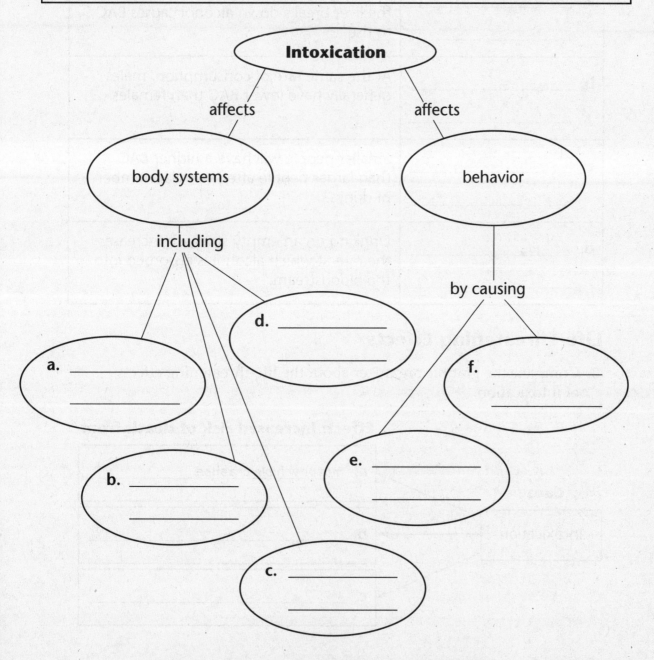

Name _____ Class _____ Date _____

Section 15-2: **Note Taking Guide** (continued)

Blood Alcohol Concentration

2. Complete the table about the factors that affect a drinker's blood alcohol concentration. Use the phrases from the box below.

> Rate of consumption   Gender
>
> Amount of food in the stomach   Body size

Factor	Why It Affects BAC
a. _____ _____	Drinking faster than the rate at which the liver breaks down alcohol causes BAC to rise.
b. _____ _____	At the same rate of consumption, males generally have lower BAC than females.
c. _____ _____	Smaller people will have a higher BAC than larger people after a similar number of drinks.
d. _____ _____	Drinking on an empty stomach increases the rate at which alcohol is absorbed into the bloodstream.

Life-Threatening Effects

3. Complete the graphic organizer about the life-threatening effects of intoxication.

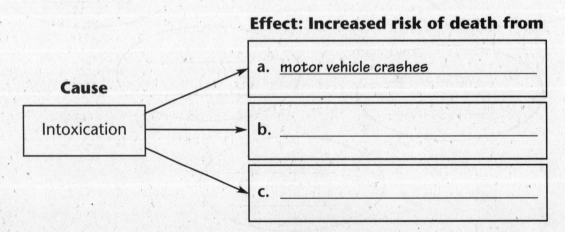

Effect: Increased risk of death from

Cause

Intoxication

a. _motor vehicle crashes_____

b. _____

c. _____

Section 15-3 **Summary**

Long-Term Risks of Alcohol (pp. 386–391)

Damage to the Body

Key Concept: **Long-term alcohol abuse may harm the brain, liver, heart, and digestive system. Drinking any amount of alcohol during pregnancy may permanently harm the developing baby.**

- Alcohol abuse can

  - destroy nerve cells in the brain. The damage can affect memory, concentration, and judgment.

  - lead to **fetal alcohol syndrome,** a group of birth defects, including brain damage, caused by the effects of alcohol on a fetus.

  - cause **cirrhosis** (sih ROH sis), a disease of the liver.

  - cause increased blood pressure and irregular heartbeat.

  - lead to cancers within the digestive system.

Alcoholism

Key Concept: **What begins as problem drinking can become absolute dependence and, finally, late-stage alcoholism.**

- **Alcoholism** is a disease in which people can no longer control their use of alcohol.

- **Tolerance** occurs with repeated use of alcohol. The effects of alcohol become reduced with repeated use. The drinker will consume more to achieve the original effect.

- With **dependence,** the brain develops a chemical need for alcohol. It cannot function normally without it.

- With **addiction,** the drinker no longer has control over his or her drinking.

- **Reverse tolerance** is a condition seen in late-stage alcoholics in which they need less and less alcohol to become intoxicated.

Treating Alcoholism

Key Concept: **There are three stages in an alcoholic's recovery: acknowledging the problem, detoxification, and rehabilitation.**

- **Detoxification** involves removing all alcohol from a person's body.

- **Withdrawal** is a group of symptoms that occur when a dependent person stops taking a drug. Alcoholics suffer from withdrawal as detoxification occurs.

- **Rehabilitation** is the process of learning to cope with everyday living without alcohol.

- Support groups can help during the recovery process.

Name _____ Class _____ Date _____

Note Taking Guide

Long-Term Risks of Alcohol (pp. 386–391)

Damage to the Body

1. Complete the table about the effects of alcohol use on the body. Use the phrases from the box below.

| Liver | Brain | Digestive system | Heart |

Organ or Body System	Effect of Alcohol Use
a. _____	destroys nerve cells; impairs memory and ability to concentrate
b. _____	interferes with liver's ability to break down fats; fills liver with fat and scar tissue
c. _____	increases blood pressure and causes irregular heartbeat; builds up fatty deposits in heart muscle
d. _____	increases risk of mouth, tongue, or stomach cancer; causes recurring diarrhea

Name _____ Class _____ Date _____

Section 15-3: **Note Taking Guide** (continued)

2. Complete the graphic organizer about the effects of fetal alcohol syndrome. Choose the terms and phrases from the box below.

delayed growth	obesity
mental retardation	malformed face

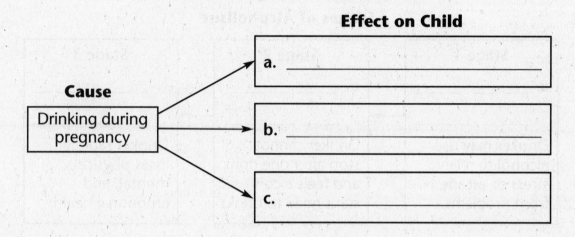

Cause

Drinking during pregnancy

Effect on Child

a. _____

b. _____

c. _____

Alcoholism

3. Complete the concept map about alcoholism.

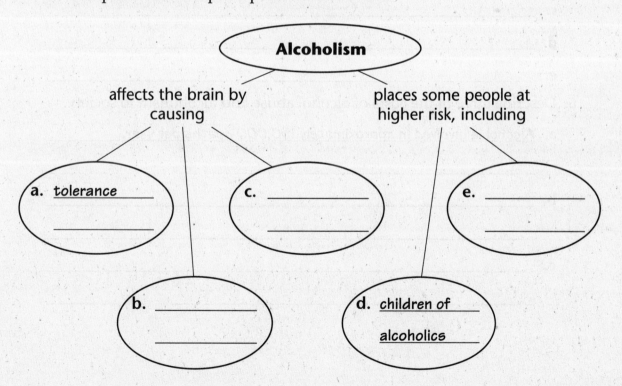

Alcoholism

affects the brain by causing

places some people at higher risk, including

a. tolerance

c. _____

e. _____

b. _____

d. children of alcoholics

Name _____ Class _____ Date _____

Section 15-3: **Note Taking Guide** (continued)

4. Complete the flowchart about the stages of alcoholism. Use the terms and phrases from the box below.

> Absolute Dependence   Problem Drinking
>
> Late Stage

Stages of Alcoholism

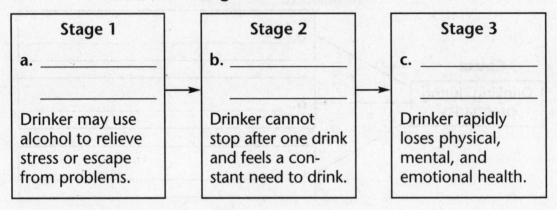

Stage 1	Stage 2	Stage 3
a. _____ _____ Drinker may use alcohol to relieve stress or escape from problems.	**b.** _____ _____ Drinker cannot stop after one drink and feels a constant need to drink.	**c.** _____ _____ Drinker rapidly loses physical, mental, and emotional health.

5. List five possible effects of alcoholism on families.

a. <u>violence</u> _____

b. <u>neglect</u> _____

c. _____

d. _____

e. _____

6. Describe three of the costs of alcohol abuse and alcoholism to society.

a. <u>Alcohol is involved in approximately 150,000 deaths per year.</u>

_____

b. _____

_____

c. _____

_____

Section 15-3: **Note Taking Guide** (continued)

Treating Alcoholism

7. Complete the flowchart about the stages in recovering from alcoholism. Use the terms and phrases from the box below.

| Rehabilitation | Detoxification | Acknowledging the Problem |

Stages in Treating Alcoholism

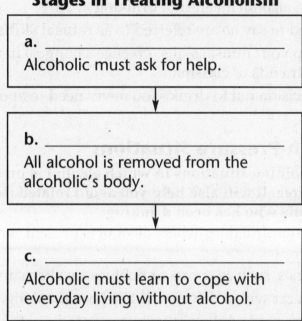

a. _____
Alcoholic must ask for help.

b. _____
All alcohol is removed from the alcoholic's body.

c. _____
Alcoholic must learn to cope with everyday living without alcohol.

8. Complete the table about three support groups that address problems of alcoholism. Use the names from the box below.

| Al-Anon | Alateen | Alcoholics Anonymous |

Support Group	Purpose
a. _____	offers encouragement and support to help alcoholics stop drinking
b. _____	helps adult friends and family members learn to help the alcoholic recover
c. _____	provides help for teenagers living with alcoholics

Section 15-4 ## Summary

Choosing Not to Drink (pp. 392–394)

Abstaining From Alcohol

Key Concept: Sticking to your decision not to drink means being able to say no with confidence in situations where other people are drinking.

- Abstaining from alcohol means not drinking at all.
- The skills needed to say *no* are referred to as **refusal skills.**
- You can develop your refusal skills. Practice saying *no* in role-playing situations with friends or classmates.
- Stick to your decision not to drink. You never need to apologize for not drinking.

Avoiding High-Pressure Situations

Key Concept: Avoiding situations in which alcohol is present will help you stay alcohol free. It will also help you avoid related risks, like being injured by someone who has been drinking.

- Staying away from situations where alcohol is present can help you stay alcohol free.
- Try other activities, such as sports or hobbies, as alternatives to parties.
- Never get into a car with a driver who has been drinking.
- Call a parent, a trusted adult, or a taxi if you need a safe ride home.

Section 15-4 Note Taking Guide

Choosing Not to Drink (pp. 392–394)

Abstaining From Alcohol

For questions 1–3, put a check mark next to the best answer.

1. What are refusal skills?

    a. _____ skills needed to say no

    b. _____ skills needed to refuse to answer

2. How can you prepare to resist being pressured to drink?

    a. _____ practice arguing skills   **b.** _____ role-play refusal skills

3. What if others do not accept your decision not to drink?

    a. _____ stick to your decision   **b.** _____ apologize

Avoiding High-Pressure Situations

4. Complete the concept map about ways to avoid pressure situations involving alcohol. Use the terms and phrases from the box below.

sports	volunteering
playing an instrument	call for help

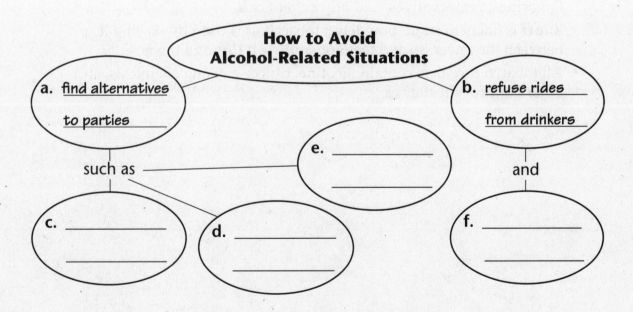

Section 16-1 Summary

Teens and Tobacco (pp. 400–403)

Why Teens Use Tobacco

Key Concept: **Friends, family, and the media greatly influence whether someone starts to use tobacco.**

- Tobacco use has fallen sharply. It is not as acceptable as it once was because people associate health problems with its use.

- Most people who become addicted to tobacco start using it during their teen years.

- A person's decision to smoke or not is influenced by friends, family, and the media.

- Tobacco advertising is highly regulated, but tobacco companies still spend $15 billion a year for advertising.

Tobacco Products

Key Concept: **Tobacco users take in nicotine whenever they use cigarettes, cigars, pipes, or smokeless tobacco products.**

- **Nicotine** is an addictive chemical in tobacco products.

- Tobacco products that are smoked include cigarettes, *bidis*, *kreteks*, cigars, and pipe tobacco.

- Tobacco that is meant to be chewed, placed between the lower lip and teeth, or sniffed through the nose is called **smokeless tobacco.**

- **Chewing tobacco** is poor-quality ground tobacco leaves mixed with flavorings, preservatives, and other chemicals.

- **Snuff** is finely ground, powdered tobacco. It is used by placing it between the lower lip and teeth or sniffing it through the nose.

- All tobacco products contain nicotine, cancer-causing chemicals, and other harmful substances.

188-201

Section 16-1 Note Taking Guide

Teens and Tobacco (pp. 400–403)

Why Teens Use Tobacco

1. Complete the table with details about how friends, family, and the media influence a teen's decision whether to use tobacco.

Influence on Tobacco Use	Positive Influence	Negative Influence
Friends	a. Teens whose friends do not smoke are less likely to smoke.	b. Teens whose friends do smoke are more likely to smoke.
Family	c. _____ _____	d. _____ _____
Media	e. _____ _____	f. _____ _____

Tobacco Products

2. Complete the concept map with details about tobacco products.

Tobacco Products

smoked products — are classified as → a. _____ _____

both contain the drug

such as → c. _____ _____

b. _____ _____

such as → d. _____ _____

671 334 41 91

Chapter 16 Building Health Skills

Examining Advertising Tactics (pp. 404–405)

Advertisements are designed to appeal to the potential users of a product. Their purpose is to increase existing sales, and to encourage buyers to switch brands. Looking at the tactics used to sell a product helps you resist the pressure of advertising.

1. **Identify the tactics being used to sell the product.**

   Explain how each tactic could influence a potential buyer.

   a. Humor _____

   _____

   b. Slogans and jingles _____

   _____

   c. Testimonials _____

   _____

   d. Attractive models _____

   _____

   e. Positive images _____

   _____

   f. Bandwagon approach _____

   _____

   g. Appeal to the senses _____

   _____

   h. Price appeal _____

   _____

Examining Advertising Tactics (continued)

2. Identify the ad's target audience.

Explain how the following characteristics of an ad could be used to target a specific audience.

a. Setting of the ad _____

_____

b. Actions of the characters _____

_____

c. Placement of the ad _____

_____

3. Identify the ad's message.

Explain one tactic you can use to identify an ad's message.

_____

_____

_____

Section 16-2 **Summary**

Chemicals in Tobacco Products (pp. 406–409)

Nicotine and the Body

Key Concept: **The major short-term effects of nicotine use are increased heart rate, increased blood pressure, and changes in the brain that may lead to addiction.**

- Nicotine is a type of stimulant. **Stimulants** are drugs that increase the activity of the nervous system.

- First-time tobacco users may show signs of mild nicotine poisoning, including a rapid pulse, clammy skin, nausea, and dizziness. In frequent tobacco users, nicotine stimulates parts of the brain that produce feelings of reward and pleasure.

- People who use nicotine frequently first develop a tolerance and later an addiction to nicotine.

- Tobacco users may develop a dependence on nicotine for psychological reasons.

- Nicotine addicts who go without nicotine may go through nicotine withdrawal.

Other Dangerous Chemicals

Key Concept: **In addition to nicotine, two of the most harmful substances in tobacco smoke are tar and carbon monoxide.**

- **Tar** is the dark, sticky substance that forms when tobacco burns. Tar causes short-term and long-term health damage to the body.

- Tar contains many chemicals that are **carcinogens** (kahr SIN uh junz), or cancer-causing agents.

- When tobacco is burned, an odorless, poisonous gas called **carbon monoxide** is produced. Carbon monoxide binds to red blood cells and prevents them from carrying oxygen.

- Smokeless tobacco contains many of the same dangerous chemicals that are in tobacco smoke. A smokeless tobacco user absorbs more nicotine with each dose than a person smoking a cigarette.

Section 16-2 Note Taking Guide

Chemicals in Tobacco Products (pp. 406–409)

Nicotine and the Body

1. What are two effects of nicotine on each of the following body systems?

   a. Respiratory system <u>increases mucus production, decreases muscle</u>

   <u>action in airway</u> _____

   b. Nervous system _____

   _____ .

   c. Cardiovascular system _____

   _____ .

   d. Digestive system _____

   _____ .

2. List the symptoms of nicotine withdrawal.

   <u>headaches,</u> _____

   _____

Name _____ Class _____ Date _____

Section 16-2: **Note Taking Guide** (continued)

Other Dangerous Chemicals

3. Complete the graphic organizer with details about harm resulting from tar and carbon monoxide in tobacco smoke. Use the phrases from the box below.

increased breathing and heart rate	more respiratory infections
paralysis of cilia in airways	impaired lung function
shortage of oxygen	

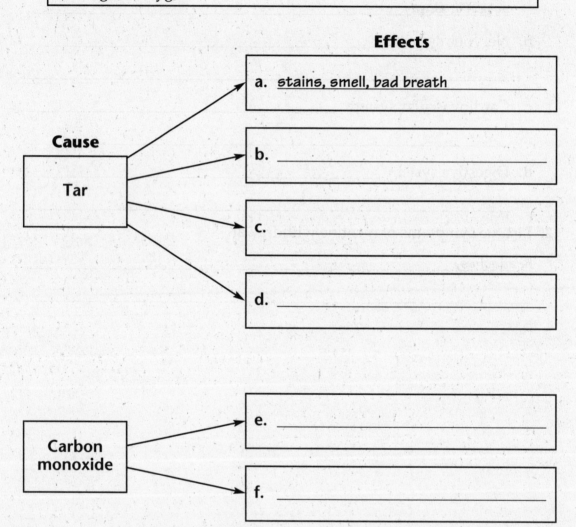

Effects

Cause

Tar

a. <u>stains, smell, bad breath</u>

b. _____

c. _____

d. _____

Carbon monoxide

e. _____

f. _____

Section 16-3 *Summary*

Risks of Tobacco Use (pp. 410–416)

Long-Term Risks

Key Concept: Tobacco use increases a person's risk of developing respiratory diseases, cardiovascular disease, and many cancers.

- Tobacco use is the leading cause of preventable death in the United States.

Respiratory Diseases

Key Concept: If a person continues to smoke over a long period of time, the damage that occurs to the respiratory system becomes permanent.

- **Chronic obstructive pulmonary disease (COPD)** is a disease that results in a gradual loss of lung function.
- With **chronic bronchitis,** the airways are constantly inflamed.
- **Emphysema** is a disorder in which alveoli lose function.

Cardiovascular Disease

Key Concept: The combined effects of nicotine, tar, and carbon monoxide force the cardiovascular system to work harder to deliver oxygen throughout the body.

Cancer

Key Concept: Tobacco use is a major factor in the development of lung cancer, oral cancers, and several other cancers.

- Lung cancer is the leading cause of cancer death.
- Tobacco users may develop white patches called **leukoplakia** (loo koh PLAY kee uh) on their tongues or the lining of their mouths.

Secondhand Smoke

Key Concept: Long-term exposure to secondhand smoke can cause cardiovascular disease, many respiratory problems, and cancer.

- **Mainstream smoke** is exhaled from a smoker's lungs. **Sidestream smoke** goes directly into the air from a cigarette. **Secondhand smoke** is a combination of mainstream and sidestream smoke.

Tobacco Use and Pregnancy

Key Concept: Pregnant women who smoke put their babies at risk for many health problems.

- Babies born to mothers who smoke are more likely to have low birthweights.
- Pregnant women who smoke are more likely to have miscarriages, premature births, and stillbirths.

Section 16-3 Note Taking Guide

Risks of Tobacco Use (pp. 410–416)

Long-Term Risks

1. What three serious health problems are associated with long-term use of tobacco?

   a. _____

   b. _____

   c. _____

Respiratory Diseases

2. Complete the graphic organizer about the effects of chronic bronchitis and emphysema. Use the phrases from the box below.

alveoli lose shape and elasticity	inflamed airways
area for gas exchange is reduced	over-production of mucus

Effects

Cause

Chronic bronchitis

a. _____
_____

b. _____
_____

Emphysema

c. _____
_____

d. _____
_____

Name _____ Class _____ Date _____

Section 16-3: **Note Taking Guide** *(continued)*

Cardiovascular Disease

3. Complete the table about increased risks of cardiovascular disease to smokers compared to nonsmokers. Use the words or phrases from the box below.

| stroke | circulation problems | heart attack |

Type of Cardiovascular Disease	Increased Risk to Smokers
a. _____	two to three times
b. _____	two times
c. _____	ten times

Cancer

4. Complete the graphic organizer about cancers linked to tobacco.

Main Idea: Tobacco is a major factor in the development of lung cancer, oral cancers, and several other cancers.

a. _____	b. _____	c. _____
leading cause of cancer deaths; 15 percent of patients survive for more than five years	includes cancers of the mouth, tongue, and throat; about 90 percent are linked to tobacco use	additional risk for cancers of the esophagus, larynx, stomach, pancreas, kidney, bladder, and blood

Section 16-3: **Note Taking Guide** (continued)

Secondhand Smoke

5. Classify each example as mainstream smoke, sidestream smoke, or secondhand smoke.

   a. Rises directly from cigarette

   sidestream smoke _____

   b. Exhaled from smoker's lungs

   _____

   c. Long-term exposure can cause serious diseases

   _____

   d. Some tar and nicotine is trapped

   _____

   e. Contains twice as much tar and nicotine

   _____

   f. Especially harmful to children

   _____

Tobacco Use and Pregnancy

6. Complete the graphic organizer about tobacco use and pregnancy. Use the phrases from the box below.

low birthweight	increases heart rate	slows cell growth
SIDS	reduces oxygen	lifelong health problems

Main Idea: Pregnant women who smoke put their babies at risk for many health problems.

Effect on Developing Baby

a. _____

b. _____

c. _____

Risk to Baby Following Birth

d. _____

e. _____

f. _____

Name _____ Class _____ Date _____

Section 16-4 *Summary*

Saying No to Tobacco (pp. 417–420)

Avoiding Tobacco Use

Key Concept: Sticking to your decision not to use tobacco involves being able to say no clearly and with confidence.

• Deciding not to use tobacco will help you stay healthy now and reduce your risk of developing life-threatening diseases in the future.

• Do not assume you can start smoking now and then quit. Studies show that people who start using tobacco in their teens have a more difficult time quitting than people who start using tobacco as adults.

Benefits of Quitting

Key Concept: The health benefits of quitting tobacco use begin immediately and continue throughout life. Society also benefits every time a tobacco user quits.

• Quitting tobacco use lowers blood pressure and heart rate immediately. In time, circulation improves and the risk of heart disease and stroke become similar to that of nonsmokers.

• Quitting smoking allows the cilia in air passages to regain normal function and breathing to become easier.

• People who quit smoking usually have increased confidence.

• Quitting smoking benefits society by reducing healthcare costs for tobacco-related illnesses.

Tips for Quitting

Key Concept: The most important factor in successfully quitting tobacco is a strong personal commitment.

• Quitting smoking is most difficult within the first week or two after the last cigarette.

• After a few weeks, symptoms of nicotine withdrawal subside, but psychological symptoms may continue.

• Many resources are available to help tobacco users who are trying to quit, such as workshops or online counseling.

• A **nicotine substitute** is a product that contains nicotine, but not the other harmful chemicals found in tobacco. Use of a nicotine substitute makes it possible for a person to reduce withdrawal symptoms when quitting tobacco.

Section 16-4

Note Taking Guide

Saying No to Tobacco (pp. 417–420)

Avoiding Tobacco Use

1. What is one example of how you can say no to a cigarette or other tobacco product offered to you?

_____

Benefits of Quitting

2. Complete the graphic organizer about the benefits of quitting tobacco. Use the terms from the box below.

| Psychological Benefits | Respiratory Benefits |
| Cardiovascular Benefits | Benefits to Society |

a. _____
blood pressure decreases; circulation improves; risk of heart disease and stroke decrease

b. _____
breathing becomes easier; cilia regain normal function

Benefits of Quitting Smoking

c. _____
increased confidence; feeling of regained control

d. _____
lower healthcare costs; reduced expenses from fire injuries and damages; reduced loss of earnings

Name _____ Class _____ Date _____

Tips for Quitting

3. Put a check mark next to some things that a person can do to help cope with withdrawal symptoms when quitting smoking. Check all that apply.

_____ a. Make a list of reasons why you quit.

_____ b. Throw away all tobacco products and reminders of tobacco.

_____ c. Have just one cigarette every now and then.

_____ d. Change your daily routine in small ways.

_____ e. Tell family and friends that you have quit.

_____ f. Avoid being around people who use tobacco.

_____ g. Spend the money you save on a reward for yourself.

_____ h. When thinking of smoking, exercise or call a friend.

Section 17-1

Summary

Legal and Illegal Drugs (pp. 426–432)

Facts About Drug Use

Key Concept: Drug abuse occurs when people intentionally use any kind of drugs for nonmedical purposes.

- **Medicines** are legal drugs that help the body fight injury, illness, or disease.

- A medicine that is sold legally in pharmacies and other stores without a doctor's prescription is called an **over-the-counter drug.**

- A drug that can be obtained only with a written order from a doctor and can be purchased only at a pharmacy is known as a **prescription drug.**

- An **illegal drug** is a chemical substance that people of any age may not lawfully manufacture, possess, buy, or sell.

- The improper use of medicines is called **drug misuse.**

- When a drug is intentionally used improperly or unsafely, it is known as **drug abuse.**

Drug Abuse and the Brain

Key Concept: Many psychoactive drugs trigger activity along a pathway of cells in the brain called the "reward pathway."

- A mood-altering drug, also called a **psychoactive drug** (sy koh AK tiv), is a chemical that affects brain activity.

- Psychoactive drugs typically create a pleasurable feeling that the user wants to repeat. Abuse of psychoactive drugs may result in addiction.

Dangers of Drug Misuse and Abuse

Key Concept: When drugs are misused or abused, many serious health effects can result.

- A **side effect** is an unwanted physical or mental effect caused by a drug.

- A **drug antagonism** (an TAG uh niz um) occurs when two or more drugs are taken at the same time and each drug's effect is canceled out or reduced by the other.

- A **drug synergism** (SIN ur jiz um) occurs when drugs interact to produce effects greater than those that each drug would produce alone.

Legal Risks and Other Costs

Key Concept: Drug abusers risk facing serious legal penalties, damaging their relationships with family and friends, and causing significant costs to society.

- Drug abuse affects many more people than just the abusers.

Section 17-1 ## Note Taking Guide

Legal and Illegal Drugs (pp. 426–432)

Facts About Drug Use

1. Complete the table about different kinds of drugs. Use the phrases from the box below.

examples are aspirin and cough remedies	not lawful to buy or sell
obtained only with doctor's orders	also called street drugs
doctor informs patient of correct amount	

Drug	Facts
Over-the-counter drugs	a. <u>sold legally in stores without a doctor's prescription</u> b. _____
Prescription drugs	c. _____ d. _____
Illegal drugs	e. _____ f. _____

Match the description of how a medicine is being used with the correct term on the right.

2. _____ Using per doctor's instructions   **a.** Drug misuse

3. _____ Mistakenly taking more than is recommended   **b.** Proper use

4. _____ Deliberately taking more than is recommended   **c.** Drug abuse

Name _____ Class _____ Date _____

Section 17-1: **Note Taking Guide** (continued)

Drug Abuse and the Brain

5. Complete the graphic organizer about how drugs affect the brain. Use the phrases from the box below.

pleasure signal weakens	pleasure signal becomes stronger
pleasurable sensations produced	

	Cause	**Effect**
Brain under normal conditions	Dopamine travels between brain cells.	a. _____ _____
Brain on drugs	Cells release extra dopamine.	b. _____ _____
Brain after repeated drug use	Cells lose receptors for dopamine.	c. _____ _____

Section 17-1: **Note Taking Guide** (continued)

Dangers of Drug Misuse and Abuse

6. Identify each risk of drug misuse or abuse. Use the terms from the box below

Side effects	Impurities	Other health risks
Withdrawal	Drug interactions	Dependence

a. _____

The drug user experiences unwanted physical or mental effects.

b. _____

The body develops a chemical need for the drug.

c. _____

The body reacts negatively or even violently when drug use stops.

d. _____

The user experiences a dangerous drug antagonism or drug synergism.

e. _____

The drug user is harmed by chemicals contaminating some illegal drugs.

f. _____

Using needles to inject drugs, the user may get hepatitis or HIV.

Legal Risks and Other Costs

7. List three costs of drug abuse in addition to health risks.

a. legal risks _____

b. _____

c. _____

Section 17-2 *Summary*

Factors Affecting Drug Abuse (pp. 434–437)

Risk Factors

Key Concept: **A number of factors make it either more or less likely that a teen will abuse drugs. They include family factors, social factors, and personal factors.**

- Family factors, such as poor family relationships or drug abuse by family members, may make teen drug abuse more likely.

- Social factors that influence teens to use drugs include a peer group or role models who abuse drugs. Competitive pressure on athletes may lead to drug abuse as well.

- Personal factors, such as stress and low self-esteem, can also influence a teen to use drugs.

Protective Factors

Key Concept: **Having strong protective factors in your life will help you stay drug free.**

- A **protective factor** is a factor that reduces a person's potential for harmful behavior.

- Teenagers who have good relationships with their parents and other family members are better equipped to deal with life's problems and stresses.

- Strong social bonds and supports can cushion the negative effects of stress in your life and act as powerful buffers against drug use.

- With guidance from adult or peer role models, teens can learn healthy techniques for managing stress.

Section 17-2 ***Note Taking Guide***

Factors Affecting Drug Abuse (pp. 434–437)

Risk Factors

1. Complete the table about risk factors that affect drug abuse.
   Use the terms from the box below.

| Family factors | Social factors | Personal factors |

Risk Factor	Example
a. _____	poor relationships at home
b. _____	drug-abusing peer group
c. _____	low self-esteem

Protective Factors

2. Complete the graphic organizer about protective factors that help you avoid drug abuse. Use the phrases from the box below.

parental awareness	strong bonds to school
commitment to success	supportive friends
clear family rules	believe drug abuse is unacceptable

Main Idea: Having strong protective factors in your life will help you stay drug free.

Family Factors

a. _____
_____

b. _____
_____

Social Factors

c. _____
_____

d. _____
_____

Personal Factors

e. _____
_____

f. _____
_____

Chapter 17 — *Building Health Skills*

Intervening to Help a Friend (pp. 438–439)

Intervening to help a friend who abuses drugs is difficult. If you wanted to help a friend the way Jen wants to help Christina, what could you do? Use the worksheet below and on the next page to help you make a plan.

1. Talk to your friend.

   a. What specifically could you say to show your concern?

_____

_____

_____

_____

   b. What could you say to help your friend face the facts?

_____

_____

_____

_____

   c. What could you say to describe your feelings?

_____

_____

_____

_____

   d. What specific help and support could you offer your friend?

_____

_____

_____

_____

Intervening to Help a Friend (continued)

2. Ask another friend to help.

What concerns and guidelines for intervening could you give a second friend who also wants to help?

_____

_____

_____

3. Follow through.

What could you do to help your friend know that your offer of support can be counted on?

_____

_____

_____

4. Seek adult or professional help.

Under what circumstances should you ask an adult to intervene?

_____

_____

_____

5. Recognize your limitations.

How could you handle a situation in which your friend does not change behavior?

_____

_____

_____

_____

Section 17-3 **Summary**

Commonly Abused Drugs (pp. 440–447)

Depressants

Key Concept: Depressants slow body functions by decreasing heart and breathing rates and lowering blood pressure.

- A **depressant** is a psychoactive drug that slows brain and body reactions.
- Depressants may be **barbiturates** (bahr BICH ur its), CNS depressants, or opiates.
- An **opiate** (OH pee it) is made from psychoactive compounds found in the seed pods of poppy plants. **Heroin** is a synthetic opiate.

Stimulants

Key Concept: Stimulants increase heart rate, blood pressure, breathing rate, and alertness.

- A **stimulant** speeds up activities of the central nervous system.
- One class of powerful stimulants is the **amphetamines** (am FET uh meenz).
- **Methamphetamine** is a powerful stimulant related to amphetamines.
- **Cocaine** is a powerful but short-acting stimulant.

Hallucinogens

Key Concept: Hallucinogens overload the brain with sensory information, causing a distorted sense of reality.

- A **hallucinogen** (huh LOO sih nuh jun) is a drug that distorts perception, thought, and mood. LSD, psilocybin, and PCP are hallucinogens.

Marijuana

Key Concept: Marijuana is one of the most frequently abused psychoactive drugs. Its main ingredient changes the way information reaches and is acted upon by the brain.

- **Marijuana** (mar uh WAH nuh) is the leaves, stems, and flowering tops of the hemp plant *Cannabis sativa*.
- Marijuana has many side effects and is a gateway to other drugs.

Club Drugs, Inhalants, and Steroids

Key Concept: Three classes of drugs that are of growing concern in recent years are club drugs, inhalants, and anabolic steroids.

- **Club drugs** first gained popularity at dance clubs and raves.
- An **inhalant** (in HAYL unt) is a breathable chemical vapor that produces mind-altering effects.
- Anabolic steroids are synthetic drugs that are similar to testosterone.

Section 17-3
Note Taking Guide

Commonly Abused Drugs (pp. 440–447)

Depressants

1. Complete the graphic organizer about depressants. Use the terms from the box below.

CNS Depressants   Barbiturates   Opiates

Main Idea: Depressants slow body functions by decreasing heart and breathing rates and lowering blood pressure.

a. _____	b. _____	c. _____
also called sedative-hypnotics; side effects include poor coordination, decreased alertness	used to be called tranquilizers; side effects include blurred vision, dizziness, skin rash	made from poppy seeds or in a lab; side effects include nausea, drowsiness, depressed respiration

Stimulants

2. Complete the table about stimulants. Use the words from the box below.

Cocaine   Methamphetamine   Amphetamines

Drug	Long-Term Effects
a. _____	irritability; irregular heart rate; liver damage
b. _____	psychotic behavior; brain damage; heart damage; stroke
c. _____	depression; paranoia; respiratory failure

Section 17-3: **Note Taking Guide** *(continued)*

Hallucinogens

3. Complete the concept map about hallucinogens. Use the terms from the box below.

psilocybin	LSD	thought
mood	angel dust	acid
perception	shrooms	PCP

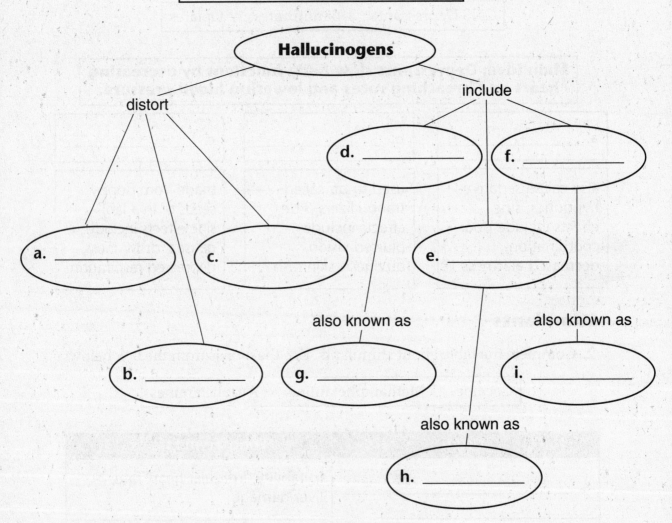

Section 17-3: **Note Taking Guide** (continued)

Marijuana

4. List three effects of marijuana use.

   a. <u>distorted perception—sights, sounds, time, and touch</u>

   b. _____

   c. _____

5. List two reasons why marijuana affects driving ability.

   a. <u>Users feel drowsy.</u>

   b. _____

6. List two reasons why marijuana is called a "gateway" to other drugs.

   a. <u>Users are in contact with dealers of other drugs.</u>

   b. _____

Club Drugs, Inhalants, and Steroids

7. Complete the outline about club drugs, inhalants, and anabolic steroids. Use the terms from the box below.

Anabolic steroids	Club drugs	Inhalants

   I. Club Drugs, Inhalants, and Steroids

   <u>Three classes of drugs that are of growing concern in recent years</u>

   <u>are club drugs, inhalants, and anabolic steroids.</u>

   A. _____

   1. Originally associated with the club scene

   2. Some kinds are associated with "date rapes"

   B. _____

   1. Include glue and household cleaners

   2. Can cause death by cardiac arrest or suffocation

   C. _____

   1. Synthetic drug similar to testosterone

   2. Can cause permanent damage to teens' bodies and brains

Section 17-4 **Summary**

Choosing to Be Drug Free (pp. 448–452)

Treating Drug Abuse

Key Concept: Treatment options for drug abusers include detoxification, therapeutic communities, and supervised medication.

- Before drug abusers can be helped, they need to recognize their problem.
- Once drug abusers recognize their problem, several treatment options are available to them.
- A person who enters a detoxification program undergoes gradual but complete withdrawal from the abused drug under medical supervision.
- A **therapeutic community** (thehr uh PYOO tik) is a residential treatment center where former drug abusers live together and learn to adjust to drug-free lives.
- A third treatment option involves replacing the abused drug with a drug that produces some of the same effects, without the "high." This also must be done under medical supervision.

Staying Drug Free

Key Concept: Practicing refusal skills, seeking help when you need it, and getting involved in drug-free activities can help you stay away from drugs.

- There are steps you can take to protect yourself from using drugs.
- Refusing drugs can be difficult when you are faced with pressure to take them. Sharpening your refusal skills can be helpful.
- If the stresses and problems in your life are too much to manage, find someone to talk to.
- There are many healthy and constructive activities that can lift your mood and help you handle the pressures in your life.
- Physical activity boosts your mood and relieves the negative effects of stress.
- Volunteering to help other people can give you a good feeling about yourself.
- Participating in a youth group can give you a sense of belonging and a connection to others.

Section 17-4 ## Note Taking Guide

Choosing to Be Drug Free (pp. 448–452)
Treating Drug Abuse

1. Complete the concept map about signs of possible drug abuse.

Behavioral Signs

a. _changes in personality_

b. _____

c. _____

d. _____

Physical Signs

e. _poor coordination_

f. _____

g. _____

Signs of Possible Drug Abuse

Social Signs

h. _friends who abuse drugs_

i. _____

j. _____

Section 17-4: **Note Taking Guide** (continued)

2. Complete the graphic organizer by filling in the three treatment options for drug abuse.

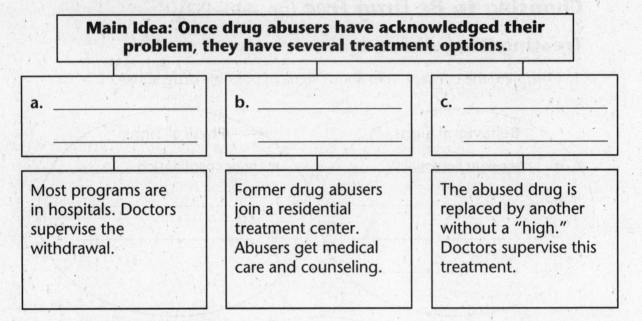

Main Idea: Once drug abusers have acknowledged their problem, they have several treatment options.

a. _____ _____

b. _____ _____

c. _____ _____

Most programs are in hospitals. Doctors supervise the withdrawal.

Former drug abusers join a residential treatment center. Abusers get medical care and counseling.

The abused drug is replaced by another without a "high." Doctors supervise this treatment.

Staying Drug Free

3. Complete the table about staying drug free. Use phrases from the box below.

| Seeking help | Refusing drugs | Finding alternatives to drugs |

Goal	Methods
a. _____ _____	Clearly state your personal reasons for not wanting to take drugs. Remove yourself from the situation.
b. _____ _____	Talk to a trusted adult. Call a national drug-abuse hotline.
c. _____ _____	Engage in physical activity. Volunteer to help others. Join a youth group.

Section 18-1 ## Summary

The Endocrine System (pp. 460–463)

What Is the Endocrine System?

Key Concept: **The endocrine system regulates long-term changes in the body such as growth and development. The endocrine system also controls many of your body's daily activities.**

- An **endocrine gland** is an organ that produces and releases chemical substances that signal changes in other parts of the body.

- A chemical substance produced by an endocrine gland is known as a **hormone.**

- A hormone is a chemical messenger. Each hormone affects certain cells in the body. These cells are its target cells.

- A hormone is carried in the blood to its target cells. When the hormone reaches its target cells, it may turn on, turn off, speed up, or slow down the activities of these cells.

Functions of Endocrine Glands

Key Concept: **The endocrine glands include the hypothalamus, pituitary gland, thyroid gland, parathyroid glands, thymus gland, adrenal glands, pancreas, and reproductive glands.**

- The **hypothalamus** (hy poh THAL uh mus) is an endocrine gland located in the brain. The hypothalamus is part of both the endocrine system and the nervous system.

- The **pituitary gland** (pih TOO ih tehr ee) is a pea-sized endocrine gland in the brain. The pituitary controls growth, reproduction, and metabolism.

- Some hormones made by the pituitary gland are like "on" switches for the body's other endocrine glands. They signal other glands to start releasing their hormones.

- Reproductive glands are part of the endocrine system.

- **Puberty** is the period of sexual development during which a person becomes sexually mature and physically able to reproduce.

- Puberty starts when the hypothalamus signals the pituitary gland to begin making hormones that cause the reproductive glands to start making sex hormones.

Section 18-1 **Note Taking Guide**

The Endocrine System (pp. 460–463)

What Is the Endocrine System?

1. What is a hormone?

   __✓__ **a.** a chemical substance produced by an endocrine gland, which acts as a chemical messenger to specific cells

   _____ **b.** an electrical impulse produced by an endocrine gland, which controls the functions of the nervous system

Functions of Endocrine Glands

2. Complete the table about the functions of endocrine glands. Use the words from the box below.

Pituitary	~~Thymus~~	~~Adrenal~~
Parathyroid	~~Thyroid~~	

Gland	Function
a. Hypothalamus	links the nervous system and the endocrine system
b. Pituitary	controls other endocrine glands and regulates growth rate
c. Thymus	regulates the body's metabolic rate and blood calcium levels
d. Thyroid	regulates levels of calcium and phosphorus
e. Thymus	helps the immune system develop
f. Adrenal	triggers the body's response to stress; affects salt and water balance

Section 18-2 **Summary**

The Male Reproductive System (pp. 464–468)

Structure and Function

Key Concept: **The functions of the male reproductive system are to produce sex hormones, to produce and store sperm, and to deliver sperm to the female reproductive system.**

- In males, the reproductive cells are called **sperm.**

- In a process called **fertilization,** a sperm cell may join with an egg.

- **Testes** are the two male reproductive glands. Testes produce sperm cells and testosterone.

- **Testosterone** is the hormone in males that affects the production of sperm. It also helps to bring about physical changes during puberty.

- The testes hang outside the main body cavity in a sac of skin called the **scrotum.**

- The **penis** is the sexual organ that sperm travel through as they leave the body.

- As they pass through the male reproductive system, sperm get mixed with fluids and form **semen.**

- **Ejaculation** is the ejection of semen from the penis.

Keeping Healthy

Key Concept: **Keeping the male reproductive system healthy involves five things—cleanliness, sexual abstinence, protection from trauma, self-exams, and regular medical checkups.**

- The penis and the scrotum should be cleaned every day.

- The best way to avoid sexually transmitted diseases in the teen years is to abstain from sexual activity.

- Males should wear a protector or cup during athletic activities.

- Males should be careful about lifting heavy objects to prevent getting a hernia.

- Males should follow up with a doctor if they notice pain when urinating, unusual discharges, sores on the genitals, or signs of testicular cancer.

- Medical exams throughout life can help ensure reproductive health. Prostate gland problems as well as prostate cancer are common after age 50.

- **Infertility** is the inability to reproduce. In males, infertility is the inability to produce healthy sperm or the production of too few sperm.

Section 18-2 Note Taking Guide

The Male Reproductive System (pp. 464–468)

Structure and Function

1. Complete the table about the structures of the male reproductive system. Use the terms from the box below.

| Vas deferens | Accessory glands |
| Epididymis | Penis |

Structure	Description and Function
a. Testes	oval-shaped male reproductive glands; hang outside the main body cavity in the scrotum; produce testosterone and sperm
b. _____	external sexual organ through which sperm leave the body
c. _____	structure where sperm mature and are stored
d. _____	tube through which sperm travel to the seminal vesicles
e. _____	glands that add fluid to sperm, producing semen

Section 18-2: **Note Taking Guide** (continued)

Keeping Healthy

2. Complete the concept map about keeping the male reproductive system healthy. Use the terms and phrases from the box below.

self-exams	medical checkups	cleanliness
protection from trauma	sexual abstinence	

a. _____
Clean external organs daily.

e. _____
Help ensure good reproductive health by seeing a doctor regularly.

Keeping Healthy

b. _____
Avoid risk of sexually transmitted infections.

d. _____
Check body for signs of medical problems.

c. _____
Wear a cup or supporter.

Section 18-3

Summary

The Female Reproductive System (pp. 469–475)

Structure and Function

Key Concept: **The functions of the female reproductive system are to produce sex hormones, to produce eggs, and to provide a nourishing environment in which a fertilized egg can develop into a baby.**

- Female reproductive cells are called eggs, or **ova.**
- The reproductive glands in which eggs are produced are called **ovaries.**
- **Estrogen** is a female sex hormone that activates certain physical changes at puberty and controls the maturation of eggs.
- **Progesterone** activates changes in the body during pregnancy.
- During **ovulation**—about once a month—an ovary releases a ripened egg.
- **Fallopian tubes** are the passageways that carry eggs away from the ovaries toward the uterus.
- The **uterus** is a hollow, muscular, pear-shaped organ. A fertilized egg can develop and grow in the uterus.
- The **vagina** is the passageway from the uterus to the outside of the body.

The Menstrual Cycle

Key Concept: **During the menstrual cycle, an ovary releases a mature egg. The egg travels to the uterus. If the egg is not fertilized, the uterine lining is shed and a new cycle begins.**

- During the **menstrual cycle,** a woman produces one mature egg cell.
- Each menstrual cycle lasts about 28 days.
- Except during pregnancy, menstrual cycles occur each month from puberty until about the age of 45 to 55, or menopause.
- At **menopause,** hormone production slows down and eggs are no longer released.

Keeping Healthy

Key Concept: **Caring for the female reproductive system involves cleanliness, sexual abstinence, prompt treatment for infections, self-exams, and regular medical checkups.**

- A woman should see a doctor about vaginal infections, unusual pain or bleeding, or if her period stops completely.
- All women who have reached puberty should have a yearly exam of the reproductive system, which may include certain tests. In a **Pap smear,** cells from the cervix are examined for cancer. A **mammogram** is an X-ray of the breasts used to detect breast cancer.

Section 18-3 Note Taking Guide

The Female Reproductive System (pp. 469–475)

Structure and Function

1. Complete the outline about the female reproductive system.

   I. Structure and Function

   A. _____

      1. produce the sex hormones estrogen and progesterone

      2. release mature egg cells

   B. _____

      1. passageways that carry eggs away from the ovaries

      2. fertilization may occur here if sperm are present

   C. _____

      1. hollow, muscular, pear-shaped organ

      2. fertilized egg develops within

   D. _____

      1. also called the birth canal

      2. hollow, muscular passage leading from the uterus

The Menstrual Cycle

2. What are four factors that may affect a woman's menstrual cycle?

   a. <u>diet</u>   c. _____

   b. <u>stress</u>   d. _____

Section 18-3: **Note Taking Guide** (continued)

3. What is meant by the term *menopause*?

_____ **a.** stage of life at which ovaries decrease hormone production and no longer release mature eggs

_____ **b.** stage of life at which ovaries increase hormone production and begin to release mature eggs

4. Complete the graphic organizer about the stages of the menstrual cycle. Use the phrases from the box below.

egg travels through fallopian tube

mature egg released during ovulation

unfertilized egg enters uterus

egg matures in ovary; uterine lining thickens

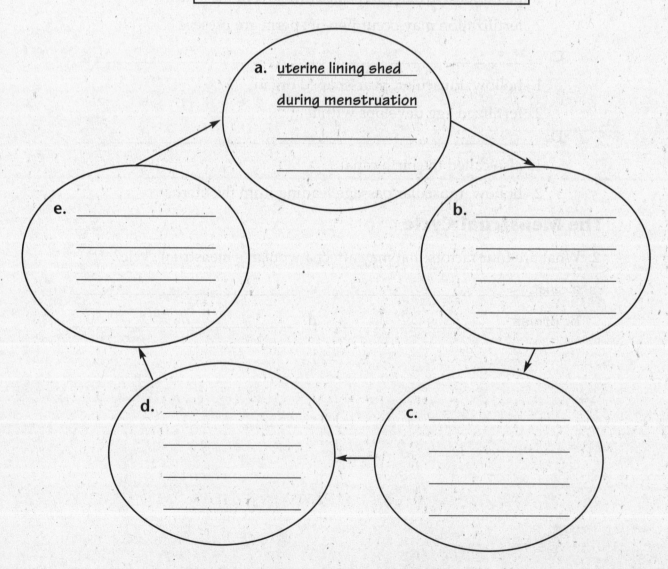

a. uterine lining shed
during menstruation
_____
_____

e. _____
_____
_____
_____

b. _____
_____
_____
_____

d. _____
_____
_____
_____

c. _____
_____
_____
_____

Name _____ Class _____ Date _____

Section 18-3: **Note Taking Guide** (continued)

Keeping Healthy

5. Complete the concept map about keeping the female reproductive system healthy. Use the terms and phrases from the box below.

medical checkups	sexual abstinence	self-exams
cleanliness	prompt treatment for infection	

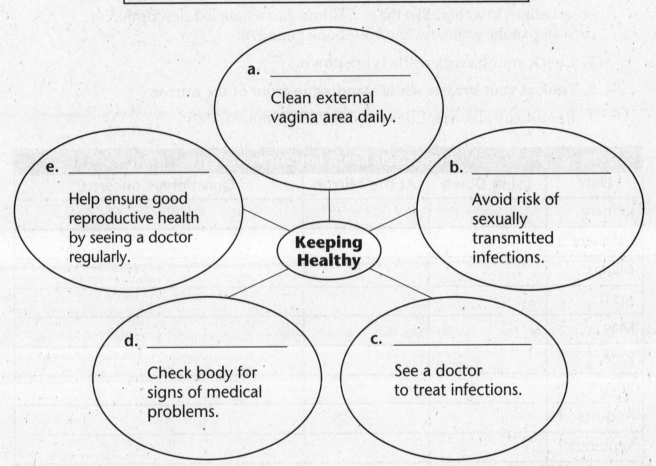

a. _____
Clean external vagina area daily.

e. _____
Help ensure good reproductive health by seeing a doctor regularly.

Keeping Healthy

b. _____
Avoid risk of sexually transmitted infections.

d. _____
Check body for signs of medical problems.

c. _____
See a doctor to treat infections.

6. Complete the table about medical tests that can help protect the health of females.

Test	Description and Purpose
Pap smear	a. _sample of cells from cervix is examined_ _____ b. _____
Mammogram	c. _____ d. _____

Chapter 18 Building Health Skills

Breast and Testicular Self-Exams (pp. 476–477)

Breast Self-Exam

The teen years are a good time to establish the habit of regular self-exams once a month. To help yourself get into the habit, you might record your observations in a chart like the one below. For a detailed description of each step of the exam, review your book page 476.

1. Check your breasts while lying down.

2. Look at your breasts while standing in front of the mirror.

3. Report any abnormalities to your doctor immediately.

Breast Self-Exam Log for Females			
Date	Lying Down	At the Mirror	Questions/Concerns
January			
February			
March			
April			
May			
June			
July			
August			
September			
October			
November			
December			

Breast and Testicular Self-Exams (continued)

Testicular Self-Exam

The teen years are a good time to establish the habit of regular self-exams. To help yourself get into the habit, you might record your observations in a chart like the one below. For a detailed description of each step of the exam, review your book page 477.

1. **Examine each testis separately with both hands.**
2. **Report any abnormalities to your doctor immediately.**

Testicular Self-Exam Log for Males		
Date	**Self-Exam Done**	**Questions/Concerns**
January		
February		
March		
April		
May		
June		
July		
August		
September		
October		
November		
December		

Name _____ Class _____ Date _____

Summary

Heredity (pp. 478–482)

The Basic Rules of Heredity

Key Concept: Hereditary information passes from one generation to the next through genes contained on the two sets of chromosomes that a person receives from their parents.

- Traits, such as eye color and the shape of ears, are caused in part by the genetic information people inherit from their parents.

- **Heredity** is the passing of biological traits from parent to child.

- **Chromosomes** are tiny structures in cells that carry information about the traits that you inherit.

- Most cells in your body contain 46 chromosomes. Sex cells, meaning sperm or eggs, contain 23 chromosomes.

- When fertilization takes place, 23 chromosomes from an egg are joined with 23 chromosomes from a sperm.

- Every chromosome is made up of genes. A **gene** is a part of a chromosome that determines a trait.

- When fertilization takes place, the fertilized egg receives two copies of each gene for a trait, one from the egg and one from the sperm.

- Some traits are either dominant or recessive and determined by two forms of a single gene. Most traits, however, are determined by many different genes, and other factors also may affect how a trait appears.

Heredity and Disease

Key Concept: Genetic disorders are caused by the inheritance of an abnormal gene or chromosome. However, for most diseases, your environment and your behavior affect your risk as much as or even more than the genes you have inherited.

- An abnormal condition caused by a gene or chromosome that is inherited is called a **genetic disorder**. Examples include cystic fibrosis, hemophilia, Huntington's disease, and Down syndrome.

- Some genes do not cause a disease but seem to increase a person's risk of getting some diseases, such as breast cancer, colon cancer, high blood pressure, and diabetes.

- Environmental risk factors such as air pollution, certain chemicals, and sun exposure may affect whether you get a disease.

- Genetic testing involves examining a person's blood for specific genes.

- Gene therapy would potentially involve giving a person copies of healthy genes to replace unhealthy ones.

Section 18-4 *Note Taking Guide*

Heredity (pp. 478–482)

The Basic Rules of Heredity

1. Complete the graphic organizer about heredity.

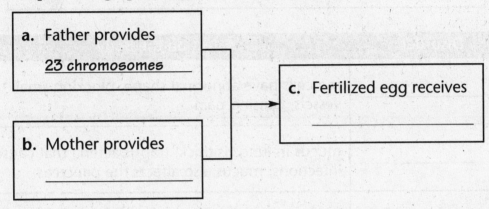

a. Father provides

23 chromosomes

b. Mother provides

_____

c. Fertilized egg receives

_____

2. What is a gene?

_____ **a.** a cell made up of several chromosomes that determine or affect a trait

_____ **b.** a section of a chromosome that determines or affects a trait

3. How do dominant and recessive traits differ?

_____ **a.** A recessive trait appears in an offspring if only one dominant form of the gene is present.

_____ **b.** A recessive trait appears in an offspring only when the dominant form of the gene is *not* present.

Section 18-4: **Note Taking Guide** (continued)

Heredity and Disease

4. Complete the table about the effect of each genetic disorder on the body. Use the terms from the box below.

| Hemophilia | Cystic fibrosis | Sickle cell disease |
| Down syndrome | Huntington's disease | |

Disorder	Effect on the Body
a. _____	red cells have abnormal shape, blocking small vessels, causing pain
b. _____	mucus in lungs is thick; traps bacteria that cause infections; mucus also affects the pancreas
c. _____	blood does not clot, leading to internal bleeding that can harm joints
d. _____	brain cells start to die in middle age; mental abilities and coordination decline
e. _____	mental retardation and heart defects; ranges from mild to severe

5. Classify each risk factor as one that you can control or as one that you cannot control.

a. fair complexion <u>*cannot control*</u>_____

b. use of tanning beds _____

c. family history of skin cancer _____

d. climate where your family lives _____

e. unprotected exposure to the sun _____

Name _____ Class _____ Date _____

Summary

Development Before Birth (pp. 488–491)

The Beginning of the Life Cycle

Key Concept: In the first week after fertilization, the fertilized egg undergoes many cell divisions and travels to the uterus.

- The moment of fertilization is also called conception. Only one sperm can fertilize an egg.

- Fertilization usually takes place in a fallopian tube.

- The united egg and sperm is called a **zygote** (ZY goht).

- After fertilization, the zygote undergoes repeated cell divisions and it travels through the fallopian tube toward the uterus.

- The growing structure is called an **embryo** (EM bree oh) from the two-cell stage until about nine weeks after fertilization.

- About five days after fertilization, the embryo reaches the uterus. By this time, the embryo is made up of a sphere of about 50 to 100 cells surrounding a hollow center. This sphere is called a **blastocyst** (BLAS tuh sist).

- The process of the blastocyst attaching itself to the wall of the uterus is called **implantation**.

Development in the Uterus

Key Concept: The amniotic sac, placenta, and umbilical cord protect and nourish the developing embryo, and later the fetus.

- The **amniotic sac** (am nee AHT ik) is a fluid-filled bag of thin tissue that develops around the embryo after implantation. The embryo floats within this sac in amniotic fluid.

- The **placenta** is the structure that develops from the attachment holding the embryo to the wall of the uterus. Within the placenta, oxygen, nutrients, and other substances move from the mother's blood into blood vessels leading to the embryo.

- The **umbilical cord** (um BIL ih kul) is a ropelike structure that develops between the embryo and the placenta. It is within this cord that blood vessels carry materials between the mother and the embryo.

- From the third month until birth, the developing human is called a **fetus**.

Section 19-1 **Note Taking Guide**

Development Before Birth (pp. 488–491)

The Beginning of the Life Cycle

1. Complete the flowchart about the early stages of pregnancy. Use the sentences from the box below.

The blastocyst reaches the uterus.

The embryo undergoes repeated cell divisions as it travels toward the uterus.

The blastocyst implants on the wall of the uterus.

The zygote travels through the fallopian tube and begins to divide.

---

a. Fertilization occurs when a single sperm is united with an egg. _____

↓

b. _____

↓

c. _____

↓

d. _____

↓

e. _____

Section 19-1: **Note Taking Guide** (continued)

Development in the Uterus

2. Complete the concept map about the structures that surround a growing embryo.

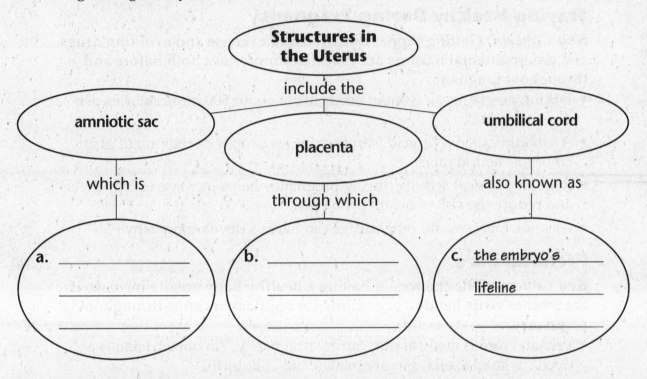

3. Complete the table about different stages of embryonic and fetal development. Use the sentences from the box below.

> Body size increases and body fat accumulates.
>
> The fetus becomes sensitive to light and sound.

Stage	Characteristics
0–2 months	a. <u>Major body systems and organs start to form.</u>
3–6 months	b. _____
7–9 months	c. _____

Section 19-2 Summary

A Healthy Pregnancy (pp. 492–496)

Staying Healthy During Pregnancy

Key Concept: Getting proper nutrition and exercise and avoiding drugs and environmental hazards are especially important both before and throughout pregnancy.

- During pregnancy, a woman needs to eat about 300 more calories per day than usual.
- A vitamin called folic acid is important for proper development of an embryo's neural tube.
- Regular physical activity during pregnancy helps increase energy levels and reduce the risk of health problems.
- Alcohol, tobacco, and other drugs can harm a developing baby.

Prenatal Care

Key Concept: The chances of having a healthy baby greatly increase if the mother visits her doctor or clinic for regular checkups throughout pregnancy.

- **Prenatal care** is medical care during pregnancy. An **obstetrician** is a doctor who specializes in pregnancy and childbirth.
- Pregnancy is divided into three periods of time called **trimesters.** Each trimester is about three months long.
- Medical tests and technology can help monitor the health of the embryo and fetus during pregnancy. An **ultrasound** uses high-frequency sound waves to create an image of the developing fetus. **Chorionic villus sampling** (CVS) is a test in which the doctor removes and tests a small piece of the developing placenta for abnormalities. **Amniocentesis** (am nee oh sen TEE sis) involves removing and testing a small amount of the amniotic fluid surrounding the fetus.
- In an **ectopic pregnancy,** the blastocyst implants in the fallopian tube or elsewhere in the abdomen, instead of in the uterus.
- The death of an embryo or fetus in the first 20 weeks of pregnancy is called a **miscarriage.** Over 20 percent of all pregnancies end in miscarriage.
- **Preeclampsia** (pree ih KLAMP see uh), also called toxemia, is a condition in which the mother has high blood pressure and high levels of protein in the urine.
- Diabetes that develops in pregnant women is called **gestational diabetes.** It is marked by high blood sugar levels.

Section 19-2 Note Taking Guide

A Healthy Pregnancy (pp. 492–496)

Staying Healthy During Pregnancy

1. Complete the table about staying healthy during pregnancy. Use the phrases from the box below.

> reduces the risk of exposure to a dangerous parasite
> reduces the risk of gestational diabetes and other complications
> eliminates the risk of fetal alcohol syndrome

Behavior	Effect
Getting enough folic acid during pregnancy	a. encourages proper neural tube, brain, and spinal cord development _____
Getting regular exercise during pregnancy	b. _____
Avoiding all alcohol during pregnancy	c. _____
Avoiding cat litter during pregnancy	d. _____

Section 19-2: **Note Taking Guide** (continued)

Prenatal Care

2. For each trimester of pregnancy, give one example of a routine procedure performed during a prenatal visit.

   a. First trimester <u>Record medical history and weight.</u> _____

   b. Second trimester _____

   c. Third trimester _____

3. List three technologies doctors may use to monitor a pregnancy.

   a. <u>ultrasound</u> _____

   b. _____

   c. _____

4. Complete the table about complications of pregnancy. Use the terms from the box below.

Miscarriage	Ectopic pregnancy	Gestational diabetes	Preeclampsia

Complication	Description
a. _____ _____	blastocyst implants in the fallopian tube, where it cannot develop; surgery is needed to remove the embryo
b. _____ _____	embryo dies in the first 20 weeks of pregnancy; usually caused by a serious genetic defect
c. _____ _____	high blood pressure, swelling of the wrists and ankles, and high levels of protein in the urine; prevents fetus from getting enough oxygen; treated with bed rest or medication
d. _____ _____	woman develops high blood sugar levels; if left untreated, fetus may grow too large.

Section 19-3 *Summary*

Childbirth (pp. 498–503)

The Birth Process

Key Concept: **Birth takes place in three stages—labor, delivery of the baby, and delivery of the afterbirth.**

- Most couples choose to have their baby in a hospital. Some couples choose to have the baby at home. A **certified nurse-midwife** is a nurse who is trained to deliver babies.

- **Labor** is the work performed by the mother's body to push the fetus out. Strong contractions of the muscles of the uterus cause the cervix to increase in width, or dilate.

- Near the end of labor the amniotic sac breaks, and the cervix becomes softer and wide enough for the fetus to pass through.

- During the actual birth, or delivery of the baby, contractions of the uterus continue to push the baby out of the mother's body. Contractions after the baby is born push out the placenta.

- The **postpartum period** is the first six weeks after the baby is born. Many changes occur to both the baby and the mother during this time.

Complications at Birth

Key Concept: **Some complications result in a surgical delivery or premature birth. Low birthweight may also cause complications.**

- Very rarely, a pregnancy may end with a stillbirth. A **stillbirth** occurs when a fetus dies and is expelled after the 20th week of pregnancy.

- A **cesarean section** (suh ZEHR ee un) is a surgical method of birth. If vaginal delivery is dangerous, a cesarean section may be done.

- A **premature birth** is the delivery of a live baby before the 37th week of pregnancy. The earlier the birth, the more problems a baby can have.

- A newborn that weighs less than 5.5 pounds at birth has a **low birthweight.** Both premature and low birthweight babies have increased risk of health problems, both as newborns and throughout life.

Multiple Births

Key Concept: **Multiple births carry a greater risk to the mother and babies and are closely monitored by doctors.**

- The delivery of more than one baby is called a **multiple birth.**

- Twins can be identical or fraternal. Identical twins develop from a single fertilized egg that divides into two identical embryos very early in development. Fraternal twins occur when two eggs are released and fertilized by two different sperm.

Section 19-3

Note Taking Guide

Childbirth (pp. 498–503)

The Birth Process

1. Complete the flowchart about the birth process. Use the sentences in the box below.

> The uterus contracts and pushes out the placenta.
>
> The uterus contracts and the cervix dilates.
>
> The baby is pushed through the cervix and vagina.

Labor

a. _____

_____

↓

Delivery of Baby

b. _____

_____

↓

Delivery of Afterbirth

c. _____

_____

2. Put a check mark next to the correct answer.

The time after birth in which the newborn and the parents adjust is called

_____ **a.** the post-birth period.

_____ **b.** the postpartum period.

_____ **c.** the afterbirth.

Section 19-3: **Note Taking Guide** *(continued)*

Complications at Birth

3. Complete the graphic organizer about complications at birth. Use the phrases from the box below. Use one phrase twice.

chronic health problems more likely	takes about 1 hour
also called a cesarean section	often lungs are not fully developed
smoking increases the risk	

Main Idea: Some complications result in a surgical delivery or premature birth. Low birthweight may also cause complications.

Surgical Delivery	Premature Birth	Low Birthweight
a. about 25 percent of all deliveries	d. delivery of live baby before the 37th week of pregnancy	g. newborn that weighs less than 5.5 pounds at birth
b. _____	e. _____	h. _____
c. _____	f. _____	i. _____

Multiple Births

4. Complete the table about the different types of twins.

Type of Twins	Description
a. _____	A single fertilized egg divides into two identical embryos early in development.
b. _____	Two eggs are released from the ovary and are fertilized by two different sperm.

Chapter 19 | *Building Health Skills*

Coping With Change (pp. 504–505)

Coping with change is something people must do throughout their lives. Using a "Change Chart" to organize your thoughts can help you cope.

1. Accept change as normal.

Think of a change that you have experienced in the recent past, are experiencing now, or are anticipating for the near future. Describe the change in the Change Chart.

2. Expect mixed feelings.

Changes bring both positive and negative feelings. Listing the advantages and disadvantages of the change can help you understand these feelings. In the Change Chart, list three advantages and three disadvantages of the change you identified in step 1.

3. Understand your resistance.

Resistance to change is normal. Here are two tips for coping with that resistance.

- Review the disadvantages you listed in your Change Chart. Identify those that are short-term and cross them out. These disadvantages will disappear as soon as you integrate the new situation into your life.

- Circle the disadvantages over which you have no control. Try to just "let go" of the things you cannot control.

Change Chart
Change : _____
Advantages
1._____
2._____
3._____
Disadvantages
1._____
2._____
3._____

Coping With Change (continued)

4. Build an inside support system.

What lessons have you learned from coping with change in the past that you can apply now?

_____

_____

_____

_____

5. Build an outside support system.

List at least three friends or family members who can offer support during the change. Then list at least one other group or organization from which you can seek support.

_____

_____

_____

_____

6. Start with small steps.

Choose a goal to focus on as you make your change. Write your goal below, and then list two small, positive steps you can take to work toward that goal.

Goal _____

Step _____

Step _____

7. Work through setbacks.

List two things you can do if you find yourself returning to your old ways or feeling scared about the change.

_____

_____

_____

Name _____ Class _____ Date _____

Summary

Childhood (pp. 506–508)

Early Childhood

Key Concept: From birth to age six, children change from helpless babies into confident individuals who can do many things for themselves.

- At birth, many of a baby's organ systems are not fully developed. The brain, nerves, and muscles are ready for more coordinated movement by the time a baby is three or four months old.

- Most children learn to talk between 18 months and 3 years of age.

- Between the ages of 3 and 6 years old, children become more independent and active. They also begin school, learn how to behave in a group, and start to develop a sense of right and wrong.

Middle to Late Childhood

Key Concept: Physical growth, mastering new skills, and making friends are key areas of development during middle and late childhood.

- Middle childhood is the period between 6 and 8 years old.

- Late childhood is the period between 9 and 12 years old. Late childhood is also called **pre-adolescence.** It is the stage of development before adolescence.

- During middle and late childhood, muscles and bones continue to grow and coordination continues to develop.

- Mental development continues during middle and late childhood. Children start to learn higher-level thinking skills and continue to learn values, such as honesty and fairness.

- Around age 10, the approval of friends and the need to fit in with a social group become very important.

Section 19-4 **Note Taking Guide**

Childhood (pp. 506–508)

Early Childhood

1. Complete the flowchart about early childhood. Use the sentences in the box below.

Child learns to talk.

Child learns to play with others.

Child learns to recognize parents and siblings.

Birth to Eighteen Months

a. Child cries for help. _____

_____

b. _____

_____

↓

Eighteen Months to Three Years

c. Baby fat is lost and arms and _____

legs get longer. _____

d. _____

_____

↓

Three to Six Years

e. Child becomes more _____

independent and active. _____

f. _____

_____

Name _____ Class _____ Date _____

Section 19-4: **Note Taking Guide** (continued)

Middle and Late Childhood

2. Complete the concept map about middle and late childhood.

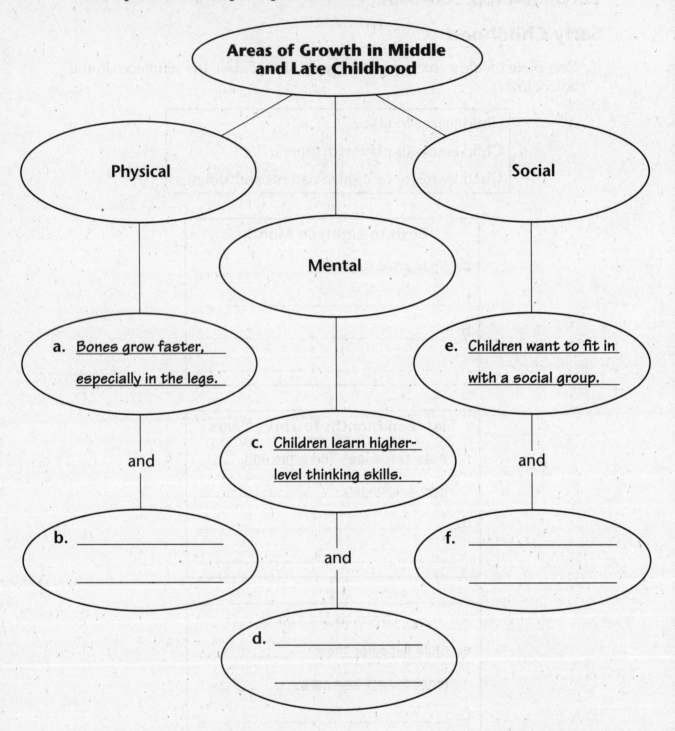

Name _____ Class _____ Date _____

Summary

Adolescence: A Time of Change (pp. 514–521)

Changes in Your Body

Key Concept: During adolescence, the reproductive system matures, adult features appear, and height and muscle mass increase.

- **Adolescence** is a period of gradual change from childhood to adulthood that occurs from about the ages of 12 to 19. Adolescence is marked by physical, mental, and emotional changes.

- Puberty is the period of time during which reproductive maturity develops. **Reproductive maturity**—the ability to produce children—is marked by the onset of sperm production in boys and ovulation in girls.

- **Secondary sex characteristics** are physical changes that develop during puberty that are not directly involved in reproduction.

- The ages at which people mature sexually and grow to their adult height are determined in part by heredity.

Mental Changes

Key Concept: Mental changes during adolescence include improved abstract thinking, reasoning skills, and impulse control.

- Mental changes that occur during adolescence are affected by changes taking place in the brain.

- Abstract thinking involves being able to consider ideas that are not concrete or visible. The improvement of abstract thinking skills in teens is accompanied by growth in the brain's frontal cortex.

- Reasoning abilities—the ways you solve problems and make decisions— increase during adolescence.

- Impulses, or tendencies to act rapidly based on emotional reactions, are affected by a part of the brain that is more active in teens than in adults. This may make it more difficult for adolescents to control their impulses.

Emotional Changes

Key Concept: During adolescence, individuals start to define meaning in their lives, a set of personal values, and a sense of self.

- Searching for meaning in life helps teens to begin to choose a way of life that is right for them.

- Values are beliefs that are important to an individual. Most people begin to establish a set of personal values during adolescence.

- Teens may search for a sense of self by experimenting with different clothing, hairstyles, and behaviors, or by exploring their racial or cultural identities.

Section 20-1 Note Taking Guide

Adolescence: A Time of Change (pp. 514–521)

Changes in Your Body

1. Compare changes in the body for girls and boys during puberty by completing the Venn diagram. Write similarities where the circles overlap, and differences on the left and right sides. Use the phrases from the box below.

breasts develop	body hair appears	muscle strength increases
hair on face and chest	shoulders broaden	sperm production begins
perspiration increases	hips widen	sex hormones produced
ovulation begins	body fat increases	

Boys   **Girls**

a. _____

b. _____

c. _____

d. _____

e. _____

f. _____

g. _____

h. _____

i. _____

j. _____

k. _____

Section 20-1: **Note Taking Guide** (continued)

Mental Changes

2. Complete the concept map about structures in the brain that change significantly during adolescence. Use the phrases from the box below.

> creativity and problem-solving   physical movement
>
> planning, judgment, and memory   impulses

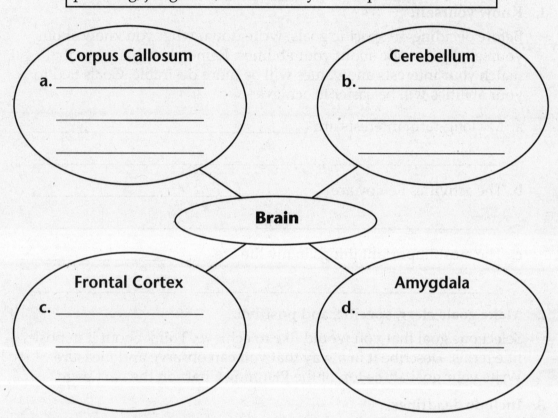

Corpus Callosum

a. _____

_____

_____

Cerebellum

b. _____

_____

_____

Brain

Frontal Cortex

c. _____

_____

_____

Amygdala

d. _____

_____

_____

Emotional Changes

3. List three things individuals begin to search for during adolescence.

a. <u>search for meaning in life</u> _____

b. _____

c. _____

Chapter 20 ## Building Health Skills

Setting a Goal (pp. 522–523)

Setting goals and achieving them is an important lifelong skill. The first step is to learn about yourself and your interests. Use this worksheet to help you set a goal and chart your progress toward that goal.

1. **Know yourself.**

   Before deciding on specific goals, write down what you know about yourself. Be realistic about your abilities. Remember that goals that match your interests and values will be more desirable. Goals tied to your abilities will be easier to achieve.

   a. My long-term interests are _____

   _____.

   b. The activities I enjoy are _____

   _____.

   c. The most important things in my life are _____

   _____.

2. **Make goals clear, specific, and positive.**

   Select one goal that you would like to achieve. Think about it in positive terms. Describe it in a way that you can observe and measure. Write your goal at the top of the Planning Chart on the next page.

3. **Include deadlines.**

   Review your goal. Does it have a deadline? If not, decide on a reasonable time limit and add it to your goal.

4. **Break long-term goals into small steps.**

   Break your goal into smaller, more manageable steps and enter these on the chart.

5. **Keep written goals visible.**

   Refer to your chart each day. Make notes in the appropriate box each day to indicate your progress toward each step.

6. **Evaluate your progress.**

   At the end of one week, review your progress and modify the steps if necessary. Work through another week and evaluate your progress again.

Name _____ Class _____ Date _____

Setting a Goal (continued)

Planning Chart

My goal is _____.

Deadline _____

Steps	Week 1						
	Mon.	Tues.	Wed.	Thur.	Fri.	Sat.	Sun.
1.							
2.							
3.							
4.							
5.							

Planning Chart

My goal is _____.

Deadline _____

Steps	Week 2						
	Mon.	Tues.	Wed.	Thur.	Fri.	Sat.	Sun.
1.							
2.							
3.							
4.							
5.							

Name _____ Class _____ Date _____

Section 20-2 *Summary*

Adolescence and Responsibility (pp. 524–528)

Responsibilities to Yourself

Key Concept: **Your pathway to adulthood will be marked by a growing responsibility for your own decisions and actions.**

- During adolescence you begin to become responsible for taking care of yourself.
- Many decisions that teens face can affect their health and safety. Eventually teens need to learn to make decisions and resist negative influences on their own.
- Adolescence is a time to begin planning for the future.

Responsibilities to Others

Key Concept: **Your responsibilities to your family, friends, and community increase greatly during adolescence.**

- Family friction may result from differences among a teen's **autonomy**, or independence, and his or her roles and responsibilities in the family.
- Increased independence often comes with increased responsibilities.
- Friendships become very important during adolescence. Being a good friend involves being helpful, being a good listener, and offering comfort and encouragement when needed.
- During adolescence, many teens develop a sense of responsibility to the community. This involves following community rules, becoming interested in public issues, and giving back to the community in various ways.

Section 20-2 Note Taking Guide

Adolescence and Responsibility (pp. 524–528)

Responsibilities to Yourself

1. Complete the table about responsibilities to yourself. Use the phrases from the box below.

Resisting negative influences	Thinking about your future
Making everyday decisions	

Responsibility	Description
a. _____ _____	During adolescence you become responsible for taking care of yourself.
b. _____ _____	Following irresponsible behaviors of peers can have serious consequences. You need to make your own decisions and take responsibility for the results.
c. _____ _____	Adolescence is a time to begin planning for your future and making decisions that can help you keep your options open.

Name _____ Class _____ Date _____

Section 20-2: **Note Taking Guide** (continued)

Responsibilities to Others

2. Complete the outline about your responsibilities to others during adolescence. Use the phrases from the box below.

Responsibility to community	Your role in the family
Responsibility to friends	Responsibility to family

I. Responsibilities to Others

   A. _____

   1. you gain greater independence from family

   2. parents may value family's ways more than your autonomy

   B. _____

   1. helping out around the house

   2. giving back through understanding and support to other family members

   3. playing by the rules of the family

   C. _____

   1. willingness to take time from activities to help out a friend

   2. being a good listener

   3. offering comfort and encouragement when needed

   D. _____

   1. learning and obeying the laws of the community

   2. recognizing how your actions might affect the community

   3. helping to find ways to improve the community

Section 20-3 Summary

Adulthood and Marriage (pp. 529–536)

Young Adulthood

Key Concept: You will change physically and emotionally during the transition from adolescence into young adulthood. In fact, changes continue throughout your life as an adult.

- Most people reach **physical maturity,** the state of being full-grown in the physical sense, by their late teens or early twenties.

- Adults reach **emotional maturity,** or full development in the emotional sense, over their lifetime.

Marriage

Key Concept: Love, compatibility, and commitment are key factors in a successful marriage.

- Approximately 90 percent of Americans marry at some time in their lives.

- People marry for different reasons, including love and companionship, financial security, social or cultural reasons, and starting a family.

- Changes in attitudes and expectations and unexpected problems can cause stress in a marriage. Effective communication is an important tool in helping a couple get through difficult times.

- One part of a couple's decision to become parents should include consideration of the financial demands of raising a child.

- When teenagers marry, they often face more difficulties than those who marry later.

Healthy Aging

Key Concept: People tend to reduce or delay the physical signs of aging when they establish healthy behaviors during their youth.

- Physical changes associated with aging include graying hair, facial wrinkles, reduced vision and hearing, slowed reflexes, brittle bones, and a need for the heart to work harder.

- Men and women born today live longer than ever before. Men born today can expect to live about 75 years and women about 80 years.

- Some common diseases of adulthood include arthritis, osteoporosis, Parkinson's disease, dementia, and Alzheimer's disease.

- **Dementia** (dih MEN shuh) is a disorder characterized by loss of mental abilities, abnormal behaviors, and personality changes.

- **Alzheimer's disease** (AHLTS hy murz) causes brain cells to die, resulting in the gradual loss of mental and physical function.

Section 20-3 Note Taking Guide

Adulthood and Marriage (pp. 529–536)

Young Adulthood

1. List three signs of physical maturity.

   a. <u>body systems are fully developed</u>

   b. _____

   c. _____

2. List three signs of emotional maturity.

   a. <u>develop close relationships with others</u>

   b. _____

   c. _____

3. What three questions should a young adult consider when beginning to plan for a career?

   a. <u>What type of career will feel productive and satisfying?</u>

   b. _____

   c. _____

Section 20-3: **Note Taking Guide** (continued)

Marriage

4. Complete the table about marriage. Use the phrases from the box below.

| Stresses in marriage | Teens and marriage | Successful marriages |
| Parenthood | Why people marry | |

Main Idea	Details
a. _____ _____	people desire another person's love and companionship; for financial, social, or cultural reasons; to start a family
b. _____ _____	love, friendship, commitment, compatibility, mutual respect, physical attraction, ability to compromise
c. _____ _____	changes in attitudes or expectations; unexpected problems such as illness, loss of a job, or an unplanned pregnancy
d. _____ _____	commit to a lifetime of love, guidance, and attention to children; provide food, clothing, medical care, and other needs of children
e. _____ _____	strains of adjusting to a new relationship while earning a living and completing education; changes in friendships

Section 20-3: **Note Taking Guide** (continued)

Healthy Aging

5. Complete the graphic organizer with details about the effects of aging.

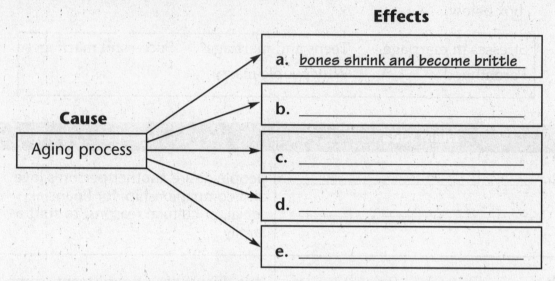

6. Complete the table about common diseases of older adulthood.

Disease	Description
a. Arthritis	disease that attacks the body's joints and makes simple tasks painful
b. _____	causes bones to break easily and heal slowly due to lack of calcium
c. _____	affects nervous and muscular systems; causes stiff muscles, shaky movements, and loss of muscle function
d. _____	causes loss of mental abilities, abnormal behaviors, and personality changes
e. _____	causes brain cells to die, resulting in gradual loss of mental and physical function

Section 20-4 *Summary*

Death and Dying (pp. 537–540)

Dying with Dignity

Key Concept: **The five stages of dying are denial, anger, bargaining, depression, and acceptance.**

- Death is part of the normal cycle that all living things go through.

- In the past most people died in their homes, surrounded by family and friends. Today, a person is more likely to die in a nursing home or hospital than at home.

- A **hospice** (HAHS pis) is a facility or program that provides physical, emotional, and spiritual care for dying people and support for their families. Most hospice workers, except for the medical personnel, are volunteers.

- A **terminal illness** is an illness for which there is no chance of recovery.

- People suffering from terminal illness, and their loved ones, typically go through five emotional stages: denial, anger, bargaining, depression, and acceptance.

Coping Skills

Key Concept: **Staying actively involved in a dying loved one's life will help both you and the dying person cope.**

- There are coping skills for dealing with a dying loved one. They include visiting the person often, listening to what the dying person has to say, not being shy about discussing death, and talking about your plans and hopes.

Key Concept: **After the death of a loved one, it is important not to deny your feelings. However, don't become so overwhelmed with emotion that you forget to care for yourself.**

- Try to talk about your loss with family and friends.

- Continue your usual routine as much as possible.

- Allow yourself time to grieve.

- You can help others through their grief by being a good listener, writing a sympathy note, helping with everyday errands, and helping them get counseling if needed.

Section 20-4 Note Taking Guide

Death and Dying (pp. 537–540)

Dying With Dignity

Coping Skills

1. Complete the outline about dying with dignity and coping skills. Use the phrases from the box below.

> Emotional support   Care for the dying   Grieving after death
> Stages of dying   Helping others through their grief

I. Dying With Dignity

   A. _____

      1. In the past, most people died at home, surrounded by family.

      2. Today, most people die in a hospital or nursing home.

      3. A hospice provides care for dying people and support for their families.

   B. _____

      1. A terminal illness is an illness from which there is no chance of recovery.

      2. There are five stages of dying: denial, anger, bargaining, depression, and acceptance.

II. Coping Skills

   A. _____

      1. Stay actively involved in a dying loved one's life.

      2. Visit often; listen; don't be shy about discussing death; talk about your plans.

   B. _____

      1. Don't deny your feelings; take care of yourself.

      2. Try to talk about your loss; try to follow your routine; allow time to grieve.

   C. _____

      1. Be a good listener; write a sympathy note; help with errands.

      2. Help the person get counseling if necessary.

Name _____ Class _____ Date _____

Summary

Understanding Infectious Diseases (pp. 548–551)

Causes of Infectious Diseases

Key Concept: Pathogens can cause an infectious disease when they enter your body and multiply.

- Organisms or viruses that enter and multiply within the human body can cause **infectious diseases** (in FEK shus).
- **Microorganisms** are organisms that are so small that they can be seen only through a microscope.
- Microorganisms and viruses that cause disease are called **pathogens.** There are many kinds of pathogens.
- **Bacteria** are simple, single-celled microorganisms. Some bacteria injure cells by giving off poisons called **toxins** (TAHK sinz).
- The smallest pathogens are **viruses.** Viruses can multiply only after entering a living cell.
- **Fungi** (FUN jy) are organisms such as yeasts, molds, and mushrooms. Fungi grow best in warm, dark, moist areas.
- **Protozoans** (proh tuh ZOH unz) are single-celled organisms that are much larger and more complex than bacteria.
- Other pathogens include mites, lice, and certain worms.

How Pathogens Are Spread

Key Concept: Pathogens can spread through contact with an infected person; an infected animal; contaminated objects; or contaminated food, soil, or water.

- Contact with an infected person can be direct, such as a handshake. Contact can also be indirect, such as sneezing.
- Infected animals can transmit disease by biting a person.
- Some pathogens can survive outside the body. These pathogens can spread from person to person through objects that are touched, such as doorknobs or eating utensils.
- Food, soil, or water may contain pathogens that are naturally present. They may also become contaminated by pathogens from infected people.

Section 21-1 Note Taking Guide

Understanding Infectious Diseases (pp. 548–551)

Causes of Infectious Diseases

1. Complete the table with details about the different kinds of pathogens. Use the terms and phrases from the box below.

can multiply only within a living cell	amebic dysentery
single-celled organisms more complex than bacteria	influenza
simple, single-celled microorganisms	ringworm
grow best in warm, dark, moist places	food poisoning

Pathogen	Description	Examples of Disease
Bacteria	a. _____ _____ _____	b. tetanus c. _____ _____
Viruses	d. _____ _____ _____	e. common cold f. _____ _____
Fungi	g. _____ _____ _____	h. athlete's foot i. _____ _____
Protozoans	j. _____ _____ _____	k. malaria l. _____ _____

Section 21-1: **Note Taking Guide** (continued)

How Pathogens Are Spread

2. Complete the concept map about how pathogens are spread. Use the
   words and phrases from the box below.

infected animals	sneezing
contaminated objects	doorknobs
cholera from water	direct contact
contaminated food, soil, or water	

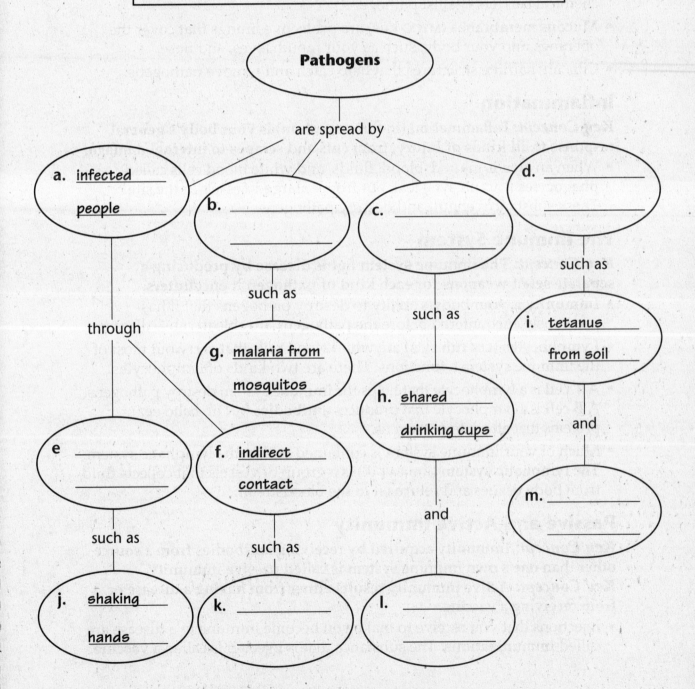

Section 21-2

Summary

Defenses Against Disease (pp. 552–557)

Physical and Chemical Defenses

Key Concept: Your body's first line of defense against infectious disease includes both physical and chemical defenses that prevent pathogens from entering your body.

- Your skin, saliva, tears, and digestive system serve as both physical and chemical barriers against pathogens.

- **Mucous membranes** (MYOO kus) are protective linings that cover the openings into your body, such as your mouth, eyes, and nose.

- Cilia are hairlike structures that help catch and remove pathogens.

Inflammation

Key Concept: **Inflammation** (in fluh MAY shun) **is your body's general response to all kinds of injury, from cuts and scrapes to internal damage.**

- When an area is injured, blood, fluids, and white blood cells called **phagocytes** (FAG uh syts) leak out from enlarged vessels at the site. These substances engulf and destroy pathogens.

The Immune System

Key Concept: **The immune system fights disease by producing a separate set of weapons for each kind of pathogen it encounters.**

- **Immunity** is your body's ability to destroy pathogens that it has previously encountered before the pathogens are able to cause disease.

- **Lymphocytes** (LIM fuh syts) are white blood cells that carry out most of the immune system's functions. There are two kinds of lymphocytes.

- A **T cell** is a lymphocyte that helps the immune system destroy pathogens. A **B cell** is a lymphocyte that produces **antibodies** (AN tih bahd eez), proteins that attach to pathogens.

- Much of your immune system is contained within the lymphatic system. The **lymphatic system** (lim FAT ik) is a group of vessels that collects fluid from body tissues and returns it to the bloodstream.

Passive and Active Immunity

Key Concept: **Immunity acquired by receiving antibodies from a source other than one's own immune system is called passive immunity.**
Key Concept: **Active immunity results either from having a disease or from receiving a vaccine.**

- Injections that you receive to make you become immune to a disease are called **immunizations**. The substance that is injected is called a **vaccine**.

Section 21-2 Note Taking Guide

Defenses Against Disease (pp. 552–557)

Physical and Chemical Defenses

1. Complete the table about the body's first line of defense against pathogens. Use the terms from the box below.

Cilia	Digestive system	Mucous membranes	Saliva and tears

Barrier	Physical Defense	Chemical Defense
a. Skin _____ _____	keeps pathogens out with surface cells that are hard and have no gaps	acid in sweat kills many bacteria
b. _____ _____	mucus traps pathogens	chemicals attack pathogens
c. _____ _____	move mucus to the mouth and nose	
d. _____ _____	trap pathogens and wash them away	contain chemicals that attack pathogens
e. _____ _____	normal motions move pathogens out of the body	acids, chemicals, and bacteria kill many pathogens

Section 21-2: **Note Taking Guide** (continued)

Inflammation

2. In what two ways does inflammation help protect the body? Choose the correct sentences from the box below.

It fights infection.	It promotes the healing process.
It produces antibodies.	It provides active immunity.

a. _____

b. _____

The Immune System

3. Label the main steps of the immune response in the diagram. Use the sentences from the box below.

B cells make antibodies.	Killer T cells attack.
A helper T cell recognizes a virus.	Antibodies destroy viruses.

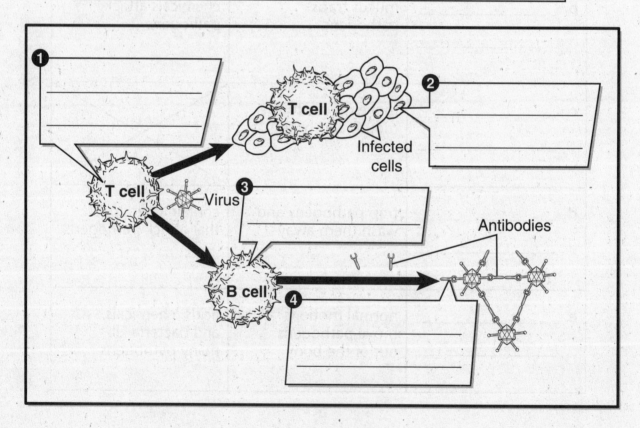

Section 21-2: **Note Taking Guide** (continued)

Passive and Active Immunity

4. Compare passive and active immunity by completing the Venn diagram. Write similarities where the circles overlap, and differences on the left and right sides. Use the phrases from the box below.

> results from having a disease or getting a vaccine
>
> provides temporary immunity
>
> may provide lifelong immunity
>
> results from receiving antibodies

Passive Immunity **Active Immunity**

a. _____

_____

_____

b. _____

_____

_____

c. help protect against infection

d. _____

_____

_____

e. _____

_____

_____

Section 21-3 ## Summary

Common Infectious Diseases (pp. 558–563)

Bacterial Diseases

Key Concept: **Four infectious diseases caused by bacteria are strep throat, Lyme disease, meningitis, and tuberculosis.**

- Strep throat is common among teenagers. Symptoms include sore throat, swollen lymph nodes, headache, and fever.
- The bacteria that cause Lyme disease can infect humans who are bitten by infected ticks. One symptom is a red rash at the site of the bite.
- Bacterial meningitis is an infection of the fluid in the spinal cord and surrounding the brain. Early treatment may prevent serious illness or death.
- Tuberculosis (too bur kyuh LOH sis) is a highly contagious infection of the lungs. Symptoms may not occur for years.
- Bacterial diseases may be treated with antibiotics. An **antibiotic** (an tih by AHT ik) is a drug that inhibits or kills bacteria.

Viral Diseases

Key Concept: **Viral diseases include the common cold, influenza, pneumonia, and hepatitis.**

- The common cold is really a group of symptoms. It is caused by a number of viruses. Colds spread through contact with an infected person.
- Influenza, or the flu, is an infection of the upper respiratory system. It can cause more serious symptoms than a cold, including a high fever.
- Pneumonia (noo MOHN yuh) is a serious lung infection. It can be caused by influenza.
- Hepatitis (hep uh TY tis) is an inflammation of the liver. The three most common types are hepatitis A, B, and C.
- Most viral infections cannot be cured by medication. Antibiotics do *not* work against viruses.

Getting Healthy, Staying Healthy

Key Concept: **If you are worried about your health for any reason, see a doctor. You can protect yourself from infectious diseases with three behaviors.**

- Avoid contact with pathogens.
- Make sure that your immunizations are current.
- Choose healthful behaviors, such as washing your hands often.

Section 21-3 *Note Taking Guide*

Common Infectious Diseases (pp. 558–563)

Bacterial Diseases

Viral Diseases

1. Complete the outline about common infectious diseases. Use the terms from the box below.

Lyme disease	Hepatitis	Influenza
Pneumonia	Tuberculosis	Bacterial meningitis

I. Bacterial Diseases

  A. Strep throat _____

    1. Symptoms: sore throat, swollen lymph glands, headache, fever

    2. Diagnosis: swab throat and identify bacteria

  B. _____

    1. Spread by: bite of infected tick

    2. Symptoms: red rash at site of bite, fever, chills, body aches

    3. Protection: wear long pants, shirts with long sleeves

  C. _____

    1. Description: infection of fluid surrounding the brain

    2. Symptoms: high fever, vomiting, headache, stiff neck

    3. Severity: can cause serious illness and death

  D. _____

    1. Description: highly contagious infection of the lungs

    2. Spread by: sneezes or coughs

    3. Symptoms: fatigue, weight loss, mild fever, constant cough

  E. Treating bacterial diseases _____

    1. Treatment: antibiotics

Section 21-3: **Note Taking Guide** (continued)

Outline (continued)

II. **Viral Diseases**

    A. <u>The common cold</u>

        1. Description: group of symptoms caused by different viruses

        2. Symptoms: sneezing, sore throat, runny nose, fever, congestion

        3. Spread by: touching contaminated object or inhaling droplets

    B. _____

        1. Description: viral infection of the upper respiratory system

        2. Spread by: touching contaminated object or inhaling droplets

        3. Symptoms: high fever, sore throat, headache cough

        4. Prevention: immunization

    C. _____

        1. People at risk: the elderly; people with heart or breathing problems

        2. Description: serious infection of the lungs

    D. _____

        1. Description: group of viruses that infect the liver

        2. Symptoms: fever, nausea, pain in abdomen, jaundice

        3. Types: A, B, and C

    E. <u>Treating viral diseases</u>

        1. Treatment: rest, well-balanced diet, plenty of fluids

Getting Healthy, Staying Healthy

2. For which condition listed below should you seek medical care?

    _____ **a.** breathing difficulties

    _____ **b.** a temperature of 99°F for one day

3. Which behavior listed below can help you avoid infectious diseases?

    _____ **a.** staying up late

    _____ **b.** cooking and storing foods properly

Chapter 21 *Building Health Skills*

Using Medicines Correctly (pp. 564–565)

For medicines to be safe and effective, you must use them according to their directions. Suppose that your doctor has prescribed an antibiotic to treat your strep throat. Use the information on the medicine label below and from your book to answer the questions that follow.

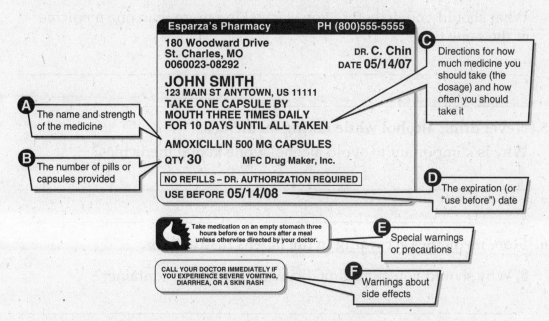

1. **Read all the information on the label and follow the directions.**

   a. What is the name of this antibiotic? What is the strength?

   _____

   b. For how long should John Smith continue taking this antibiotic?

   _____

   c. If John Smith forgets to take a dose of medicine, what should he do?

   _____

   _____

2. **Only take medicines prescribed for you.**

   Why should you not use medicines prescribed for someone else?

   _____

   _____

Using Medicines Correctly (continued)

3. **Call your doctor if a medicine causes serious side effects.**

   What are some possible side effects of this medicine?

   _____

   _____

4. **Never combine medicines without checking with your doctor.**

   What should you do before you start taking more than one medicine at the same time?

   _____

   _____

5. **Never drink alcohol while taking medicines.**

   Why is it important to avoid alcohol while taking medicines?

   _____

   _____

6. **Store medicines according to the label's instructions.**

   a. Why should you store a medicine in its original container?

   _____

   _____

   b. When should you get rid of medicines?

   _____

   _____

   c. Why should you be careful to dispose of medicines properly?

   _____

   _____

Section 21-4 Summary

Emerging Infectious Diseases (pp. 566–568)

What Is an Emerging Disease?

Key Concept: **An emerging disease is an infectious disease that has become increasingly common in humans within the last 20 years or threatens to become more common in the near future.**

- An **epidemic** (ep uh DEM ik) is an unusually high occurrence of a disease in a certain place at a certain time.
- If an epidemic affects many areas of the world, it may be called a *pandemic.*
- Some of the diseases that cause epidemics today are known as **emerging diseases.**
- Some emerging diseases are the avian flu, SARS (Severe Acute Respiratory Syndrome), yellow fever, dengue fever, and West Nile virus.

Why Do Diseases Emerge?

Key Concept: **Diseases can emerge when humans come into contact with infected animals; pathogens become resistant to existing drugs; or people lack appropriate immunizations. In addition, the increased frequency of international travel and a global food supply can enable emerging diseases to spread very quickly.**

- Avian flu is an emerging disease caused by birds.
- Diseases can become drug resistant because the pathogens mutate, or change, over time.
- In some parts of the world, people have not received vaccines. This means that they are not protected from some diseases.
- World travelers who carry pathogens can spread the pathogen around the world in a short amount of time.
- Pathogens in foods that travel around the world can cause disease outbreaks. Mad cow disease is an infectious disease that was spread by contaminated beef distributed to several countries.

Section 21-4 / Note Taking Guide

Emerging Infectious Diseases (pp. 566–568)

What Is an Emerging Disease?

1. Put a check mark next to the best answer.

   An infectious disease that has become increasingly common in humans within the last 20 years or threatens to become more common in the near future is known as

   _____ **a.** an emerging disease.   _____ **b.** a pandemic.

Why Do Diseases Emerge?

2. Complete the table about the factors responsible for emerging diseases. Use phrases from the box below.

| Global food supply | Lack of immunization | International travel |
| Contact with infected animals | Drug resistance | |

Factor	Examples
a. _____ _____	Avian flu can spread through contact with infected birds.
b. _____ _____	Antibiotic-resistant tuberculosis strains can lead to a tuberculosis outbreak.
c. _____ _____	Lack of polio vaccines in Africa and Asia can lead to a polio outbreak.
d. _____ _____	World travelers who carry pathogens can spread the pathogen around the world.
e. _____ _____	Eating contaminated meat imported from foreign countries can lead to disease outbreaks.

Name _____ Class _____ Date _____

Summary

The Risks of Sexual Activity (pp. 574–577)

The Silent Epidemic

Key Concept: There are several risky behaviors that account for the current STI epidemic. These behaviors include ignoring the risks of sexual activity, having sexual contact with multiple partners, and not getting proper treatment when necessary.

- Any pathogen, or disease-causing agent, that spreads from one person to another during sexual contact is called a **sexually transmitted infection,** or **STI.** These infections are sometimes called sexually transmitted diseases (STDs).

- STIs are harmful for several reasons. Physically and emotionally, they cause pain, discomfort, and embarrassment. They also increase the chances of certain cancers and infertility. More than $10 billion is spent in the United States each year for problems related to STIs.

- Many STIs can be treated with medicine, but some are incurable. People do not develop immunity to STIs. They can get new infections again and again.

- Many people who are sexually active do not take precautions against infection.

- The more sexual partners a person has, the greater his or her chances of getting an STI.

- If a person does not seek treatment for an STI, the chances are good that the person will spread the STI to others.

Avoiding STIs

Key Concept: Healthy behaviors such as practicing abstinence, avoiding drugs, and choosing responsible friends are ways to avoid STIs.

- The most certain way to avoid STIs is to practice sexual abstinence. Sexual abstinence means not having sexual intercourse, oral sex, or anal sex.

- People who use illegal drugs or steroids can get certain STIs when they share needles that have the blood of an infected person on them.

- Alcohol and drugs affect a person's ability to think clearly. Engaging in sex when using alcohol or drugs puts a person at risk for getting STIs.

- It is easier for teens to make healthy decisions if they go out in groups and choose friends who practice abstinence and avoid drugs.

Section 22-1 # Note Taking Guide

The Risks of Sexual Activity (pp. 574–577)

The Silent Epidemic

1. List two short-term and two long-term health effects of STIs.

   a. Short-term effects _____

   _____

   b. Long-term effects _____

   _____

2. Complete the graphic organizer by identifying three risky behaviors that contribute to the STI epidemic.

Main Idea: There are several risky behaviors that account for the current STI epidemic.		
a. _____ _____	b. _____ _____	c. _____ _____
people do not take precautions against infections	increases chance of getting an STI	increases chance of spreading an STI to others

Name _____ Class _____ Date _____

Section 22-1: **Note Taking Guide** (continued)

Avoiding STIs

3. Complete the concept map about behaviors that can help people avoid STIs.

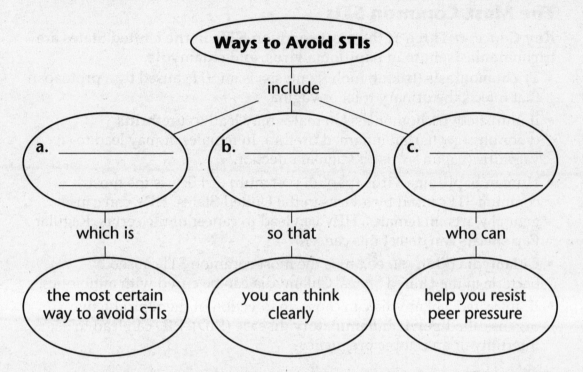

Section 22-2 **Summary**

Kinds of STIs (pp. 578–583)

The Most Common STIs

Key Concept: **Three of the most common STIs in the United States are trichomoniasis, human papilloma virus, and chlamydia.**

- **Trichomoniasis** (trik uh moh NY uh sis) is an STI caused by a protozoan that infects the urinary tract or vagina.
- If untreated, trichomoniasis in males may lead to **urethritis** (yoor uh THRY tis), an inflamed urethra. In females, it may lead to **vaginitis** (vaj uh NY tis), a vaginal infection.
- **Human papilloma virus** (pap uh LOH muh) or HPV, is the most common STI caused by a virus in the United States. HPV can cause genital warts. In females, HPV can lead to cancer of the cervix. Regular Pap smears can detect this cancer.
- **Chlamydia** (kluh MID ee uh) is the most common STI caused by bacteria in the United States. Chlamydia can be cured with antibiotics.
- If untreated, chlamydia can cause an infection of the reproductive organs called **pelvic inflammatory disease** (PID). PID can lead to infertility or an ectopic pregnancy.

Other STIs

Key Concept: **Other STIs include hepatitis, gonorrhea, genital herpes, and syphilis.**

- **Hepatitis B and C** attack the liver.
- **Gonorrhea** (gahn uh REE uh) is a bacterial STI that infects the urinary tract of males and the reproductive organs of females. Treatment requires antibiotics.
- **Genital herpes** (HUR peez) is an STI caused by a virus. There is no cure for genital herpes. During birth, it can cause blindness or death when passed to the infant.
- **Syphilis** (SIF uh lis) is a serious STI caused by bacteria. A painless sore, called a **chancre** (SHANG kur), appears in the first stage of syphilis.

Seeking Treatment

Key Concept: **People who are involved in high-risk behaviors should see a doctor every six months for a checkup. People who think they might be infected with an STI should get medical help right away.**

- People who suspect that they have an STI infection should stop all sexual activity and see a doctor.

Section 22-2

Note Taking Guide

Kinds of STIs (pp. 578–583)

The Most Common STIs

Other STIs

1. Complete the table about STIs. Use the terms from the box below.

| Human papilloma virus | Chlamydia | Hepatitis |
| Gonorrhea | Genital herpes | Syphilis |

STI	Cause	Symptoms	Treatment
a. Trichomoniasis	protozoan	itching, burning, painful urination, discharge	prescription medication
b. _____	virus	may cause genital warts	no cure, but doctor can remove genital warts
c. _____	bacteria	frequent urination and discharge in males; discharge in females	antibiotics
d. _____	viruses	fatigue, abdominal pain, nausea, and jaundice	no cure, but medication relieves symptoms
e. _____	bacteria	puslike discharge and painful urination	antibiotics
f. _____	virus	painful blisters on or around genitals	no cure, but medication relieves symptoms
g. _____	bacteria	chancre (painless sore), mouth sores, skin rash on hands and feet	antibiotics in early stages, permanent damage after second stage

Name _____ Class _____ Date _____

Section 22-2: **Note Taking Guide** (continued)
Seeking Treatment

2. Complete the flowchart with the steps to follow for treating STIs.
   Use the sentences from the box below.

> Finish all prescribed medicine.
>
> Start treatment immediately.
>
> See a doctor for an exam or blood test.
>
> Refrain from sexual activity.

Seeking Treatment for STIs

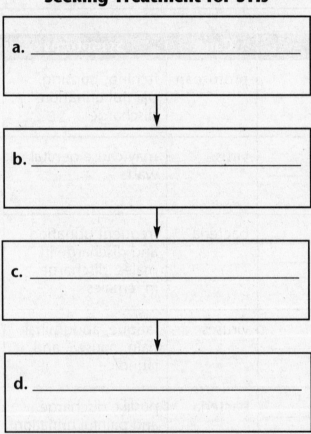

a. _____

b. _____

c. _____

d. _____

3. Why is it important that people with STIs notify their sexual partners?

_____

_____

_____

Section 22-3 **Summary**

HIV and AIDS (pp. 584–589)

HIV Infection

Key Concept: **HIV attacks specific cells in the immune system, disabling the body's defenses against other pathogens. When the immune system becomes severely disabled, the infected person has AIDS.**

- The most serious incurable STI is caused by the human immuno-deficiency virus, commonly called **HIV.**

- HIV infection can lead to **AIDS,** or acquired immuno-deficiency syndrome. An HIV infection progresses through three stages:

  ♦ The **asymptomatic stage,** when there may be no symptoms for several years.

  ♦ The symptomatic stage, when an HIV-infected person may begin to have symptoms. This stage may not occur until 7 to 10 years after infection with HIV.

  ♦ AIDS, which is marked by a very low number of helper T cells. The person's immune system is no longer able to fight off infections.

- Infections that attack a person with a weakened immune system are called **opportunistic infections.** Some opportunistic infections are tuberculosis, fungal infections, and certain kinds of pneumonia and cancers.

Transmission of HIV

Key Concept: **Individuals infected with HIV can pass the virus on to someone else through the exchange of blood, semen, vaginal fluids, or breast milk.**

- There are four main ways that HIV is spread from person to person: through sexual contact, shared needles, or contact with blood, or from mother to baby during pregnancy, birth, or breast-feeding.

- HIV is not transmitted by casual contact, such as hugging or holding hands.

- The risk of getting HIV from blood transfusions is extremely small.

A Global Problem

Key Concept: **With approximately 40 million people infected around the world, HIV and AIDS represent a global health problem.**

- The main goal of international organizations is HIV education.

- International organizations also provide medicines to millions of infected people in countries most affected by HIV and AIDS.

Name _____ Class _____ Date _____

HIV and AIDS (pp. 584–589)

HIV Infection

1. Complete the following sentence.

The fewer helper T cells that remain active in a person's body,

_____.

2. Complete the flowchart by identifying the stages of an HIV infection. Use the terms from the box below.

AIDS	Asymptomatic Stage	Symptomatic Stage

a. _____
The infected person experiences no outward signs of disease for many years. The virus destroys helper T cells.

↓

b. _____
The infected person starts to show symptoms such as weight loss, fever, diarrhea, or fungal infections.

↓

c. _____
The infected person experiences more severe symptoms, has a very low number of helper T cells, and is more susceptible to infections.

3. Put a check mark next to the correct answer.

Infections that attack a person with a weakened immune system are called

_____ **a.** lung disease.   _____ **c.** viruses.

_____ **b.** sexually transmitted infections.   _____ **d.** opportunistic infections.

Section 22-3: **Note Taking Guide** (continued)

Transmission of HIV

4. Complete the graphic organizer by identifying four ways that HIV can spread.

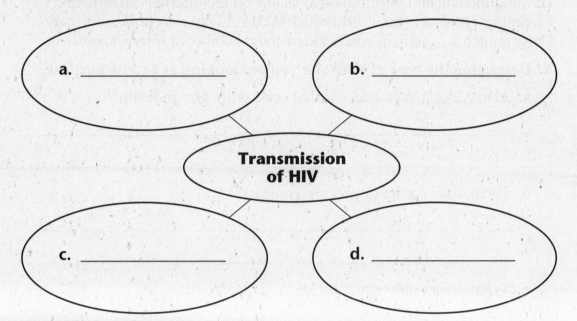

a. _____

b. _____

Transmission of HIV

c. _____

d. _____

A Global Problem

5. On which two continents are the rates of HIV and AIDS increasing most quickly?

   a. _____   b. _____

6. List two main goals of international organizations that are working to combat HIV and AIDS around the world.

   a. *educating people about HIV prevention* _____

   b. _____

Chapter 22 *Building Health Skills*

Evaluating Internet Sources (pp. 590–591)

The amount of health information available on the Internet can be overwhelming. How can you decide which Web sites have accurate information? These guidelines can help you evaluate the reliability of Internet sources.

1. Determine the type of Web site you are looking at and its purpose.

a. What does a Web address that ends with **.gov** indicate?

_____

_____

b. What does a **.com** or **.net** site indicate?

_____

_____

c. What does a **.edu** site indicate?

_____

_____

d. What does a **.org** site indicate?

_____

_____

2. Identify the author(s) of the site.

a. Where should the author of a Web site be indicated?

_____

_____

b. What information about the author should you look for?

_____

_____

_____

Evaluating Internet Sources (continued)

3. Determine if the information is current.

How can you determine if the information on a Web site is current?

_____

_____

_____

4. Determine the quality of the site.

What clues can you use to help you determine the quality of a Web site?

_____

_____

_____

5. Verify the information on the site with information from another source.

How can you verify the information on a Web site?

_____

_____

_____

Section 22-4 | Summary

Protecting Yourself From HIV and AIDS
(pp. 592–596)

Preventing HIV Infection

Key Concept: You can protect yourself from HIV by practicing abstinence, avoiding drugs, and avoiding contact with others' blood and body fluids.

- The best way to avoid HIV and AIDS is to practice sexual abstinence.
- Do not use illegal drugs and avoid sexual contact with anyone who does.
- Never share items that may have blood or other body fluids on them.
- To reduce the risk of HIV transmission, doctors, nurses, dental hygienists, and other healthcare providers practice **universal precautions.** Universal precautions include wearing gloves, gowns, and masks, and getting rid of needles properly.
- For people who are married, it is important to practice sexual fidelity. Both partners agree to have sexual contact only with one another.
- People who are sexually active can reduce the risk of HIV infection by using a latex or polyurethane condom during every sexual encounter.

Testing for HIV

Key Concept: In an HIV test, a person's blood is tested for antibodies to HIV. If antibodies are detected, a second test is done to verify the result.

- A person who is diagnosed as being infected with HIV is said to be **HIV-positive.**
- A person who is HIV-positive needs to notify all previous sexual partners so that they can be tested.
- If no antibodies appear in a person's first blood test, the person should be tested again in three months.

Treatment for HIV and AIDS

Key Concept: The main goal of HIV treatment is to keep the person's immune system functioning as close to normal as possible.

- To keep an infected person's immune system working well, treatment has to keep the person's **viral load**— the number of virus particles circulating in the body—low. Treatment must also keep the person's helper T cell count high.
- The most common treatment for HIV infection today is HAART, which stands for Highly Active AntiRetroviral Therapy.
- No one needs to be fearful of having casual contact with a person who is HIV-positive.

Section 22-4 *Note Taking Guide*

Protecting Yourself From HIV and AIDS
(pp. 592–596)

Preventing HIV Infection

1. Complete the table about ways to prevent HIV infections. Use the phrases from the box below.

Barrier protection	Avoid drugs
Sexual fidelity in marriage	Practice abstinence
Avoid contact with blood or body fluids	

Method of Prevention	Description
a. _____	avoid sexual activity; go out in groups with responsible friends
b. _____	do not inject illegal drugs; avoid sexual contact with anyone who uses illegal drugs; avoid alcohol
c. _____	never share personal items that may have blood or other body fluids on them
d. _____	both partners agree to have sexual contact only with their spouse
e. _____	use a latex or polyurethane condom during every sexual encounter

Section 22-4: **Note Taking Guide** *(continued)*

Testing for HIV

2. Complete the flowchart with details about what happens after an HIV test is performed.

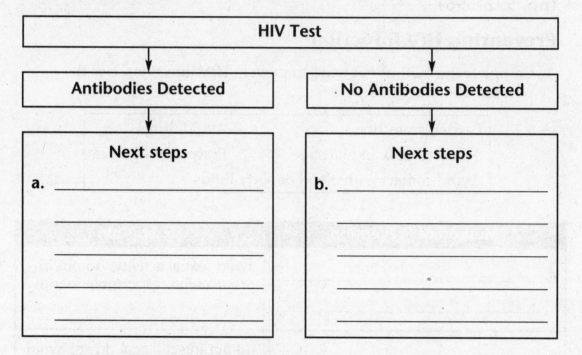

Treatment for HIV and AIDS

3. What two goals must HIV treatment accomplish in order to keep a person's immune system functioning as close to normal as possible?

   a. _____

   _____

   b. _____

   _____

4. List five healthful behaviors that people who are HIV-positive should practice.

   a. _eat right_ _____

   b. _____

   c. _____

   d. _____

   e. _____

Name _____ Class _____ Date _____

Summary

Cardiovascular Diseases (pp. 602–608)

Types of Cardiovascular Disease

Key Concept: Cardiovascular diseases include hypertension, athero-sclerosis, heart attack, arrhythmia, congestive heart failure, and stroke.

- **Chronic diseases**—diseases that persist for a long time or recur through-out life—are the leading causes of death in the United States today.

- **Cardiovascular diseases** (KAHR dee oh VAS kyuh lur) are diseases of the heart and blood vessels.

- Hypertension, or high blood pressure, can lead to heart disease.

- Atherosclerosis (ath uh roh skluh ROH sis) is a disease in which fatty substances build up inside the walls of arteries. Risk factors include a diet high in saturated fats, smoking, and lack of exercise. It can lead to arte-riosclerosis (ahr teer ee oh skluh ROH sis), or hardening of the arteries.

- Atherosclerosis in the arteries that supply the heart can lead to coronary heart disease. **Angina pectoris** (an JY nuh PEK tur is) is the chest pain that occurs when an area of the heart does not get enough oxygen-rich blood.

- A **heart attack** occurs when some of the tissue in the heart does not get its normal blood supply and dies.

- Arrhythmias are irregular heartbeats. **Fibrillation** (fib ruh LAY shun) is a life-threatening arrhythmia in which the heart twitches rapidly in an uncontrolled fashion.

- A **stroke** is a sudden disruption of blood flow to part of the brain. A **cerebral hemorrhage** (suh REE brul HEM ur ij) is a stroke that occurs in the cerebrum. One cause may be an aneurysm that bursts. An **aneurysm** (AN yuh riz um) is a blood-filled weak spot that balloons out from the artery wall.

Treating Cardiovascular Disease

Key Concept: There are many medical technologies and surgical methods available for finding and treating cardiovascular diseases.

- Testing tools include magnetic resonance imaging and electrocardiograms. Treatments include balloon angioplasty and coronary bypass surgery.

Preventing Cardiovascular Disease

Key Concept: Choosing behaviors that lower your risk for cardiovascular disease is important for your health, both now and throughout your life.

- You cannot control risk factors such as heredity, ethnicity, gender, and age.

- You can control risk factors such as maintaining a healthy weight and avoiding smoking and alcohol.

Section 23-1 Note Taking Guide

Cardiovascular Diseases (pp. 602–608)

Types of Cardiovascular Disease

1. Put a check mark next to the types of diseases that are the leading causes of death in the United States today.

_____ **a.** infectious diseases   _____ **b.** chronic diseases

2. Complete the table about cardiovascular diseases. Use the terms from the box below.

| Heart attack | Atherosclerosis | Stroke |
| Arrhythmia | Congestive heart failure | |

Disease	Description	Effect on Health
a. Hypertension	blood pressure consistently measuring 140/90 or higher	strains heart and blood vessels
b. _____	buildup of fatty substances on walls of arteries	leads to hypertension, arteriosclerosis, and heart disease
c. _____	death of tissue in heart from lack of blood	can often be fatal
d. _____	heart beats too slowly, too quickly, or irregularly	can be life-threatening
e. _____	condition in which heart slowly weakens over time	heart unable to pump as much blood as before
f. _____	sudden disruption of blood flow to part of the brain	can cause brain damage, paralysis, and death

Section 23-1: **Note Taking Guide** *(continued)*

Treating Cardiovascular Disease

3. Complete the graphic organizer about detecting and treating cardiovascular disease.

> **Main Idea: There are many medical technologies and surgical methods available for detecting and treating cardiovascular disease.**

Testing Tools

a. <u>magnetic resonance imaging</u>

b. <u>electrocardiogram</u>

c. _____

d. _____

Treatment Methods

e. <u>balloon angioplasty</u>

f. <u>coronary bypass surgery</u>

g. _____

h. _____

Preventing Cardiovascular Disease

4. List four risk factors for cardiovascular disease that you cannot control.

a. <u>heredity</u>

b. _____

c. _____

d. _____

5. List four healthy habits that can reduce your risk for cardiovascular disease.

a. <u>Maintain a healthy weight.</u>

b. _____

c. _____

d. _____

Section 23-2 *Summary*

Cancer (pp. 609–613)

How Cancer Affects the Body

Key Concept: **Cancer harms the body by destroying healthy body tissues.**

- **Cancer** is a group of diseases that involves the rapid, uncontrolled growth and spread of abnormal cells. Cancer cells typically form a mass of tissue called a **tumor.** A **malignant** (muh LIG nunt) tumor is cancerous. A benign tumor is not cancerous.

- The spread of cancer from where it first started to other parts of the body is called **metastasis** (muh TAS tuh sis).

- Cancer can be caused by hereditary factors and environmental factors. An **oncogene** (AHN kuh jeen) is a normal gene that has changed into a cancer-causing gene. A **carcinogen** (kahr SIN uh jun) is a cancer-causing agent found in the environment. Carcinogens can cause mutations in genes that control cell reproduction.

- Cancer can occur in almost any part of the body.

Detecting and Treating Cancer

Key Concept: **The key to curing cancer is early detection and treatment.**

- There are seven common warning signs of cancer that you should know: **C**hange in bowel or bladder habits; **A** sore throat that does not heal; **U**nusual bleeding or discharge; **T**hickening or lump; **I**ndigestion or difficulty in swallowing; **O**bvious change in a wart or mole; and **N**agging cough or hoarseness. Seek medical attention if you experience any of these warning signs.

- Screening tests can help detect cancer early. A **biopsy** (BY ahp see) is a procedure in which a small piece of a body tissue is surgically removed and examined for signs of cancer.

- Cancer treatments include surgery, radiation therapy, chemotherapy, and immunotherapy.

Preventing Cancer

Key Concept: **Although the specific cause of most cancers is unknown, certain behaviors have been shown to decrease the risk of cancer.**

- To reduce your risk of cancer, you should avoid tobacco and alcohol, wear protective clothing and sunscreen, choose a diet low in saturated fat and cholesterol, exercise regularly and maintain a healthy weight, avoid unnecessary X-rays, and avoid known carcinogens.

Name _____ Class _____ Date _____

Note Taking Guide

Cancer (pp. 609–613)

How Cancer Affects the Body

1. Complete the concept map about how cancer affects the body. Use the words from the box below.

biological	tumors	benign	physical
heredity	carcinogens	metastasis	

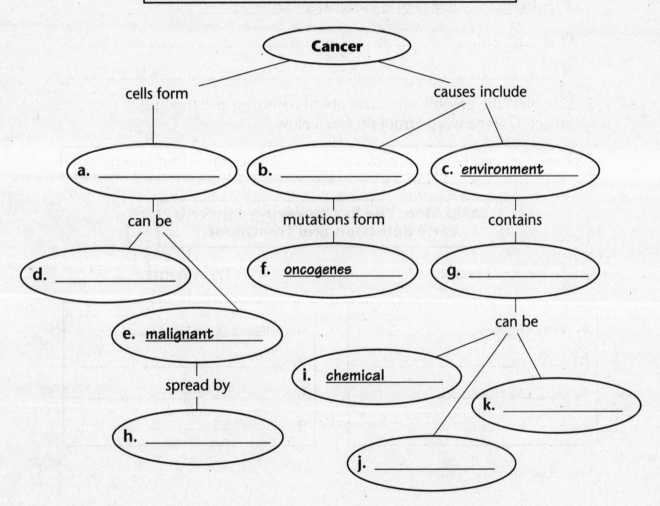

Section 23-2: **Note Taking Guide** (continued)

Detecting and Treating Cancer

2. Use the letters of the word **CAUTION** to help you list the seven warning signs of cancer.

C <u>Change in bowel or bladder habits</u>

A _____

U _____

T _____

I <u>Indigestion or difficulty in swallowing</u>

O _____

N _____

3. Complete the graphic organizer about detecting and treating cancer. Use the words from the box below.

| biopsy   chemotherapy   radiation   mammogram   immunotherapy |

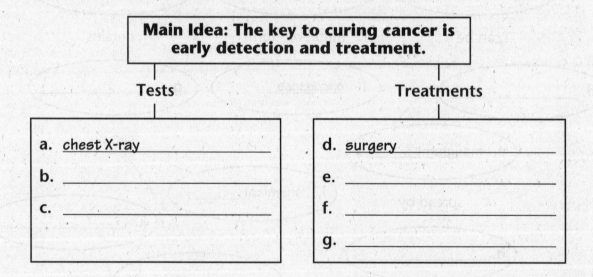

Main Idea: The key to curing cancer is early detection and treatment.

Tests

Treatments

a. <u>chest X-ray</u>

b. _____

c. _____

d. <u>surgery</u>

e. _____

f. _____

g. _____

Section 23-2: **Note Taking Guide** (continued)

Preventing Cancer

4. Complete the graphic organizer by listing behaviors that can decrease your risk of cancer.

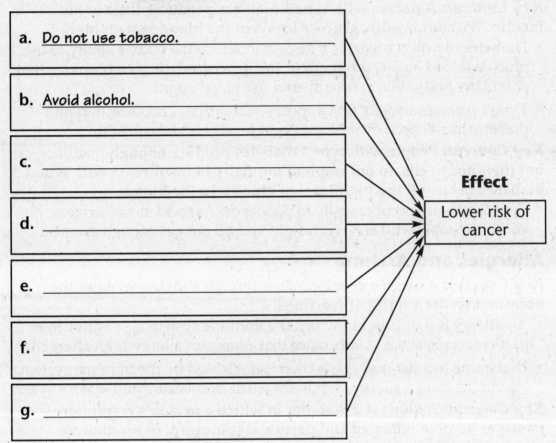

Behaviors

a. Do not use tobacco.

b. Avoid alcohol.

c. _____

d. _____

e. _____

f. _____

g. _____

Effect

Lower risk of cancer

Section 23-3 **Summary**

Other Chronic Diseases (pp. 614–619)

Diabetes

Key Concept: **A person with type 1 diabetes produces little or no insulin. Without insulin, glucose levels in the blood remain high.**

- **Diabetes** (dy uh BEE teez) is a disease in which the body's ability to use glucose (blood sugar) is impaired. **Insulin** (IN suh lin) is a hormone that stimulates body cells to take up and use blood sugar.

- Type 1 diabetes usually first appears in children. People with type 1 diabetes must check their blood sugar levels and take insulin.

Key Concept: **People with type 2 diabetes produce enough insulin, but their body cells do not respond normally to insulin. As with type 1 diabetes, the result is a high level of glucose in the blood.**

- Type 2 diabetes occurs mostly in people over age 30. It can strike younger people who are overweight and do not get enough exercise.

Allergies and Asthma

Key Concept: **Allergies develop when foreign substances enter the body and set off a series of reactions.**

- An **allergy** is a disorder in which the immune system is sensitive to a particular substance. A substance that causes an allergy is an **allergen.**

- **Histamine** (HIS tuh meen) is a chemical released by the immune system. Histamine causes allergy symptoms, such as sneezing and watery eyes.

Key Concept: **Asthma is a disorder in which a person's respiratory passages become inflamed and narrow significantly in reaction to certain "triggers."**

- Asthma can be triggered by allergens, stress, cold weather, tobacco smoke, or exercise.

- To manage asthma, people should avoid their asthma triggers and take asthma medicines.

Arthritis

Key Concept: **Arthritis results in joint stiffness, joint pain, or swelling in one or more joints.**

- **Arthritis** (ahr THRY tis) is the inflammation or irritation of a joint.

- **Osteoarthritis** (ahs tee oh ahr THRY tis) is caused by wear and tear on a joint after years of use or repeated injuries.

- In **rheumatoid arthritis** (ROO muh toid), the membrane surrounding a joint becomes inflamed. This type of arthritis affects young and old alike. Evidence shows that rheumatoid arthritis may result from the body's immune system attacking its own tissues.

Section 23-3 **Note Taking Guide**

Other Chronic Diseases (pp. 614–619)

Diabetes

1. Compare type 1 diabetes and type 2 diabetes by completing the Venn diagram. Write similarities where the circles overlap, and differences on the left and right sides. Use the phrases from the box below.

usually develops in people over 30	body produces little or no insulin
usually first appears in children	body cells do not respond normally to insulin

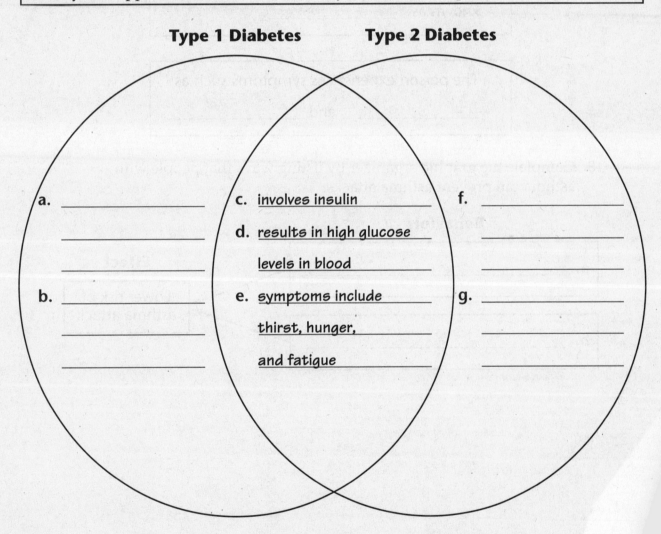

Type 1 Diabetes   **Type 2 Diabetes**

a. _____

   _____

   _____

b. _____

   _____

   _____

c. involves insulin

d. results in high glucose

   levels in blood

e. symptoms include

   thirst, hunger,

   and fatigue

f. _____

   _____

   _____

g. _____

   _____

   _____

Name _____ Class _____ Date _____

Section 23-3: **Note Taking Guide** (continued)

Allergies and Asthma

2. Complete the flowchart that describes what happens in an allergic reaction.

```
┌─────────────────────────────────────────────┐
│  a.  A person is exposed to a(n)             │
│                                              │
│      _____, such as plant pollen.│
└─────────────────────────────────────────────┘
                     │
                     ▼
┌─────────────────────────────────────────────┐
│  b.  The immune system releases a chemical   │
│                                              │
│      known as _____.             │
└─────────────────────────────────────────────┘
                     │
                     ▼
┌─────────────────────────────────────────────┐
│  c.  The person experiences symptoms such as │
│                                              │
│      _____ and _____.│
└─────────────────────────────────────────────┘
```

3. Complete the graphic organizer by listing ways that people with asthma can prevent asthma attacks.

Behaviors

```
┌─────────────────────────────────────┐
│  a.  _____   │
│                                      │        **Effect**
│                                      │
└─────────────────────────────────────┘        ┌──────────────────┐
                                     ──────────▶│  Lower risk of   │
┌─────────────────────────────────────┐         │  asthma attack   │
│  b.  _____   │──────▶  └──────────────────┘
│                                      │
└─────────────────────────────────────┘
```

Section 23-3: **Note Taking Guide** (continued)

Arthritis

4. Compare osteoarthritis and rheumatoid arthritis by completing the Venn diagram. Write similarities where the circles overlap, and differences on the left and right sides. Use the phrases from the box below.

probably caused by immune system attack	usually develops later in life
caused by wear and tear or repeated injuries	affects both young and old

Osteoarthritis   **Rheumatoid Arthritis**

a. _____

b. _____

c. causes joint stiffness, pain, or swelling

d. treatments include medicines and exercise

e. _____

f. _____

Name _____ Class _____ Date _____

Chapter 23 Building Health Skills

Being Assertive (pp. 620–621)

Think of a situation in which you wish you had acted assertively, but did not. Use this worksheet to analyze your behavior in that situation and to help you practice assertiveness skills for the future.

1. **Evaluate your current behavior.**

   _____

   _____

   _____

d. What were you afraid would happen if you acted assertively?

   _____

2. **Observe a role model in action.**

a. Describe a situation in which you saw a person act assertively.

Being Assertive (continued)

3. Conduct a mental rehearsal.

Imagine yourself being assertive in the situation this time. Describe how you would now respond with assertiveness.

_____

_____

4. Use assertive verbal behavior.

Think about what you would say. List two "I" messages you could use. Make sure the messages are specific, direct, and unapologetic.

_____

_____

5. Use assertive nonverbal behavior.

List two ways you could use body language to support your point.

_____

_____

6. Evaluate yourself.

Use this checklist to evaluate your behavior.

a. Did I say what I intended to say?	Yes	No
b. Was I direct and unapologetic, yet still considerate?	Yes	No
c. Did I stand up for myself without becoming defensive and without infringing on the other person's rights?	Yes	No
d. Was my body language assertive?	Yes	No
e. Did I feel good about myself after the encounter?	Yes	No
f. Do I think the other person felt comfortable with my interaction?	Yes	No

Name _____ Class _____ Date _____

Summary

Disabilities (pp. 623–626)

Types of Disabilities

Key Concept: **The three most common physical disabilities are impaired vision, impaired hearing, and impaired mobility.**

- A **disability** is any physical or mental impairment that limits normal activities.

- The leading causes of vision impairment in the United States are diabetes, cataracts, glaucoma, and macular degeneration. **Macular degeneration** is a condition that affects the retina. It is the leading cause of loss of vision in older Americans.

- Some vision problems can be treated with cornea transplants. People with vision impairment can use materials written in Braille, canes, and trained guide dogs.

- Causes of hearing impairment include birth defects, genetic disorders, exposure to excessive noise, and ear infections.

- **Tinnitus** is a condition in which ringing is heard in the ears, even when there is no external sound.

- Hearing aids, cochlear implants, sign language, lip reading, the Internet, and e-mail can help people with hearing impairments.

- Impaired mobility can result from disease or injury to the nervous system, muscular system, or skeletal system.

- Individuals with impaired mobility may use canes, walkers, wheel-chairs, crutches, braces, or artificial limbs to be mobile.

Living With Disabilities

Key Concept: **An important move toward integrating people with disabilities into the workplace and community came in 1990 when the Americans with Disabilities Act was signed into law.**

- People with disabilities have the same life goals as people who do not have disabilities.

- The **Americans with Disabilities Act** (ADA) guarantees the civil rights of Americans who have physical or mental disabilities.

- The ADA guarantees that people with disabilities have access to the same jobs, public services, public transportation, public accommodations and communications capabilities as everyone else.

- The Individuals with Disabilities Education Act (IDEA) of 1997 helps ensure that children with disabilities receive quality education alongside other students.

Section 23-4 **Note Taking Guide**

Disabilities (pp. 623–626)

Types of Disabilities

1. Complete the table about disabilities. Use the terms from the box below.

cochlear implants	Braille	sign language
macular degeneration	guide dogs	artificial limbs
exposure to excessive noise		

Type of Disability	Caused by	Helped by
Impaired vision	a. _diabetes_ b. _cataracts_ c. _____	d. _cornea transplants_ e. _____ f. _____
Impaired hearing	g. _birth defects_ h. _genetic disorders_ i. _____	j. _hearing aids_ k. _____ l. _____
Impaired mobility	m. _diseases_ n. _injuries_	o. _walkers_ p. _____

Living With Disabilities

2. Name the two acts that protect the rights of disabled Americans.

a. _____

b. _____

Name _____ Class _____ Date _____

Summary

The Healthcare System (pp. 634–640)

Healthcare Providers

Key Concept: **Doctors work with nurses and other healthcare providers to care for patients.**

- The **healthcare system** includes all medical services, how people pay for medical care, and programs for preventing disease and disability.
- **Primary care physicians** take care of most people's routine medical needs.
- Doctors diagnose, provide treatment, and write prescriptions for medical conditions. A **diagnosis** (dy ug NOH sis) is a doctor's opinion of the nature or cause of a medical condition.
- A **medical specialist** is a doctor who has received additional training in a particular branch of medicine.
- Other healthcare providers include nurses and healthcare professionals such as physician assistants, physical therapists, and registered dietitians.

Healthcare Facilities

Key Concept: **Healthcare facilities include doctors' offices, clinics, hospitals, and long-term care centers.**

- **Primary healthcare** is routine healthcare provided in a doctor's office.
- A patient admitted to a clinic for tests or treatment who does not need an overnight stay is an **outpatient.**
- **Secondary healthcare** is healthcare provided to a patient in a hospital. A patient who is required to stay in a hospital overnight is an **inpatient.**
- **Tertiary healthcare** is care provided in specialty or teaching hospitals.
- Long-term care facilities provide a variety of medical services.

Technology and Healthcare

Key Concept: **The Internet, e-mail, and other technologies can make healthcare more efficient. Technology can also make patients feel more involved in their care.**

- Healthcare information available on the Internet can be informative and useful, but it can also be incorrect or biased.
- Some doctors communicate with their patients via e-mail.
- MRIs, CT scans, and X-rays provide digital images that doctors can share with other specialists.
- Robot doctors allow doctors to make "virtual visits" to patients.
- Electronic health records allow doctors to share information efficiently.

Section 24-1 ## Note Taking Guide

The Healthcare System (pp. 634–640)

Healthcare Providers

1. Complete the concept map about healthcare providers. Use the terms from the box below.

physical therapists	primary care physicians	nurses
medical specialists	registered nurses	nurse practitioners
registered dietitians	other providers	

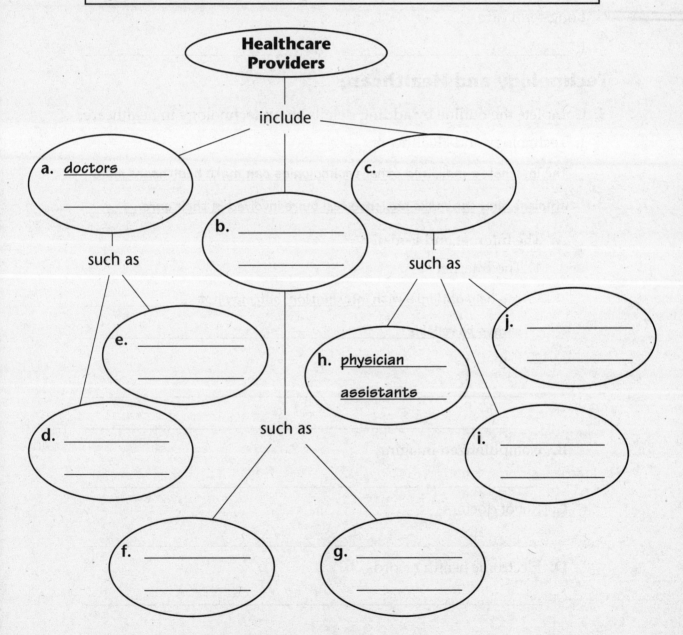

Section 24-1: **Note Taking Guide** *(continued)*

Healthcare Facilities

2. List facilities in which each type of healthcare is provided.

   Primary healthcare

   a. _doctors' offices_____   b. _____

   Secondary healthcare

   c. _____

   Tertiary healthcare

   d. _____   e. _____

   Long-term care

   f. _____   g. _____

Technology and Healthcare

3. Complete the outline by adding details about technology in healthcare.

   I. Technology and Healthcare

   The Internet, e-mail, and other technologies can make healthcare more

   _efficient, and can make patients feel more involved in their care._____

   A. The Internet and E-mail

   1. The Internet

      _can help patients with information, but may not_____

      _always be reliable_____

   2. E-mail

      _____

      _____

   B. Computerized imaging

      _____

   C. Robot doctors

      _____

   D. Electronic health records

      _____

Section 24-2 **Summary**

Participating in Your Healthcare (pp. 641–647)

Your Healthcare

Key Concept: **Deciding what doctor to see for routine healthcare deserves careful consideration. You want your healthcare delivered by qualified people with whom you feel comfortable.**

- As you grow older, you will take on the responsibility for making decisions about your healthcare.

- To find a doctor suited to your needs, ask for recommendations from family members, friends, or other healthcare providers. Once you have names, research more information about the doctor.

- At a doctor's appointment, it is important to provide your doctor with a medical history. A **medical history** is a record of your present and past health as well as that of members of your family.

- A **physical examination** is a head-to-toe check of your body to identify any medical problems you may have.

Key Concept: **As a patient you also have certain responsibilities. You must fulfill these responsibilities in order to receive the best healthcare possible.**

- As a patient you must ask your doctor about any health concerns. You must also answer your doctor's questions honestly.

Paying for Healthcare

Key Concept: **Health insurance pays for a major part of an individual's medical expenses.**

- Most health insurance plans are managed care insurance plans. In managed care insurance plans, plan members pay a monthly or yearly fee called a **premium.** A **copayment** is the small fee members may be required to pay when they visit a doctor.

- Traditional insurance plans offer more flexibility than managed care plans, but have higher out-of-pocket costs. A **deductible** is a fixed amount of money members must pay before their insurance company will begin paying for covered expenses.

- Government-sponsored health insurance programs include Medicare and Medicaid.

- Healthcare costs in the United States are rising because of an aging population, increases in the incidence of chronic diseases, and expenses due to the research and development of new drugs.

Section 24-2 ## Note Taking Guide

Participating in Your Healthcare (pp. 641–647)

Your Healthcare

1. Complete the outline with details about healthcare choices and decisions.

   I. Your Healthcare

   <u>Knowing the basics about healthcare choices can help you choose what</u>

   <u>is best for you.</u>

   A. Choosing healthcare

   <u>You need to find a qualified doctor with whom you feel comfortable.</u>

   _____

   B. Finding a doctor

   <u>Ask for recommendations.</u>

   _____

   _____

   C. The doctor appointment

   _____

   _____

   _____

   _____

   D. Your rights and responsibilities

   1. Patients' rights

   _____

   _____

   _____

   2. Patients' responsibilities

   _____

   _____

   _____

Name _____ Class _____ Date _____

Section 24-2: **Note Taking Guide** (continued)
Paying for Healthcare

2. Complete the table by identifying the type of health insurance plan described.

Health Insurance Plan	Description
a. <u>Managed care insurance</u>	a network of doctors who agree to provide healthcare to members at a lower cost; includes HMOs, POS plans, and PPOs
b. _____	members can see any doctor at any facility; out-of-pocket costs may be high
c. _____	government-run programs for people who cannot afford private insurance; include Medicare and Medicaid

Rising Healthcare Costs

3. Complete the graphic organizer about the main reasons why healthcare costs are rising.

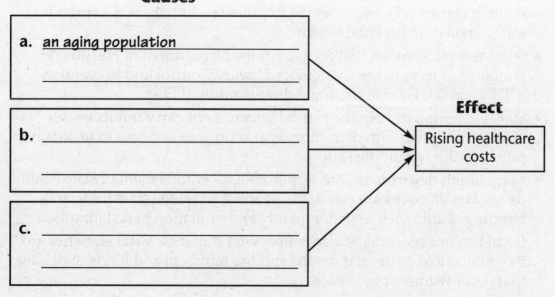

Causes

a. <u>an aging population</u>
_____

b. _____
_____

c. _____
_____

Effect

Rising healthcare costs

Section 24-3 **Summary**

Public Health (pp. 648–653)

What Is Public Health?

Key Concept: Public health programs today emphasize the need for prevention in order to avoid disease and other health problems.

- **Public health** is the study and practice of protecting and improving the health of people in a group or community.

- In the past, disease outbreaks were controlled through quarantine. **Quarantine** (KWAWR un teen) is a period of isolation imposed on people who may have been exposed to an infectious disease.

- Starting in the early 1900s, vaccines were used to reduce the incidence of many infectious diseases.

- **Epidemiology** (ep ih dee mee AHL uh jee) is the study of disease among populations. Epidemiologists use their findings to help develop policies and programs to control and prevent disease.

- Many public health problems today relate to people's behaviors. The Department of Health and Human Services, or HHS, is the major public health agency in the United States.

Public Health in the United States

Key Concept: In the United States, public health is primarily a governmental responsibility that is managed at the federal, state, and local levels.

- The three main categories into which public health programs fall are fighting chronic diseases, helping populations at risk, and improving safety and environmental health.

- Some federal agencies that are part of the Department of Health and Human Services are the Centers for Disease Control and Prevention (CDC) and the Food and Drug Administration (FDA).

- State governments help the federal government carry out its health objectives. State health departments also provide services to maintain public health within the state.

- Local health departments are responsible for enforcement of state health codes. **Health codes** are standards established by the state for factors affecting health, such as water quality and sanitation in restaurants.

- Local health departments also collect vital statistics. **Vital statistics** are the numbers of births and deaths and the numbers and kinds of diseases that occur within a population.

- Many private organizations play a role in providing healthcare services.

Section 24-3 **Note Taking Guide**

Public Health (pp. 648–653)

What Is Public Health?

1. Complete the outline with details about public health.

   I. What Is Public Health?

   <u>Public health is the study and practice of protecting and improving</u>

   <u>the health of people in a group or community.</u>

   A. The history of public health

   _____

   _____

   _____

   B. New understandings

   _____

   _____

   _____

   C. Public health goals today

   _____

   _____

   _____

Public Health in the United States

2. List the three main categories into which today's public health programs fall.

   a. <u>fighting chronic diseases</u>

   b. _____

   c. _____

Name _____ Class _____ Date _____

Section 24-3: **Note Taking Guide** *(continued)*

3. Complete the table about public health organizations and the services they provide. Use the terms from the box below.

Private organizations	Federal government
State government	Local government

Group	Services Provided
a. _____ _____	sponsor health research and education; compile and analyze health information; set health and safety standards; support state and local health departments; fund programs for people in need
b. _____ _____	carry out federal programs; distribute federal funds to local agencies or private health-service providers; provide services to maintain public health within the state
c. _____ _____	provide public health services to people; enforce state health codes; collect vital statistics
d. _____ _____	raise funds to support specific health causes; pay for medical research, health services and education programs; run programs such as food banks, counseling services, training programs, soup kitchens, and homeless shelters

Chapter 24 Building Health Skills

Working in Groups (pp. 654–655)

Choose one group to which you belong. Use this worksheet to analyze the group dynamics to understand how well its members work together.

1. Set goals and priorities.

List your group's goals in the first column of the table below. With your group, decide which goals are most important. List them in order of priority in the second column of the table.

Group Goal	Priority

2. Choose a leader.

a. Identify the leader of your group. _____

b. What qualities make this person a good leader? _____

_____

3. Delegate tasks and make a schedule.

List the tasks that the group needs to complete. Assign a group member to each task and list a date by when the task should be completed.

Task	Group Member	Date

Name _____ Class _____ Date _____

Working in Groups (continued)

4. Monitor group dynamics.

In the chart below, identify who takes on each role in your group.

Monitoring Group Dynamics	
Role	**Who plays this role in your group?**
Helpful Roles	
Starter Begins discussions; introduces new ideas	
Clarifier Requests additional information; restates points so they are clear	
Peacemaker Suggests common ground and compromise when people disagree	
Supporter Is friendly and responsive to others and their ideas	
Disruptive Roles	
Clown Uses jokes to attract attention; disrupts group	
Blocker Always disagrees with others' ideas or focuses on trivial issues	
Dominator Tries to control group; bullies other group members	

5. Evaluate group progress.

a. How well does your group work together to accomplish its tasks?

_____

_____

b. In what areas does the group need to improve in order to accomplish its goals successfully? List them here.

_____

_____

Section 24-4 *Summary*

Global Public Health (pp. 656–658)

Why Are Global Efforts Important?

Key Concept: Global efforts provide services and funding to developing nations. These nations might not otherwise have the resources to make their public health programs succeed.

- In times of crisis, people around the world work together to combat public health problems in developing nations. **Developing nations** are countries with weak economies and low standards of living.

International Health Organizations

Key Concept: International health organizations work in developing nations to overcome public health problems. These problems include malnutrition, lack of basic medical care, poor sanitation, and lack of clean water.

- The **World Health Organization** (WHO) sends people trained in medicine, agriculture, water quality, engineering, and other health-related skills to countries in need. The World Health Organization is an agency of the United Nations.

- The **United Nations Children's Fund** (UNICEF) focuses on programs that aid children. Programs include immunization programs, day-care and health centers, and school food programs. UNICEF also helps train nurses and teachers.

- The world's largest private international public health organization is the International Committee of the Red Cross. The Red Cross provides medical care, food, water, clothing, and temporary housing to victims of natural disasters anywhere in the world.

- The United States Agency for International Development (USAID) provides food and medical care to people living in developing nations.

- The Peace Corps is an agency of the U.S. government that trains volunteers for public work in developing nations.

- The governments of many countries sponsor agencies that provide international public health services.

- A number of privately supported organizations provide health services worldwide. Two examples of these organizations are Oxfam International and the Cooperative for Assistance and Relief Everywhere (CARE).

Section 24-4 *Note Taking Guide*

Global Public Health (pp. 656–658)

Why Are Global Efforts Important?

Complete the sentences below.

1. Countries with weak economies and low standards of living are

   known as _____.

2. Global public health efforts are important to developing nations

   because they _____

   _____.

International Health Organizations

3. For each organization listed below, note whether it is a United Nations agency, a privately funded organization, or a U.S. government organization. Write your response on the blank line.

   a. World Health Organization (WHO) <u>United Nations agency</u>

   b. International Committee of the Red Cross _____

   c. The Peace Corps _____

   d. Oxfam International _____

   e. The United States Agency for International Development (USAID)

      _____

   f. United Nations Children's Fund (UNICEF) _____

Section 25-1 *Summary*

Your Community, Your Health (pp. 664–669)

What Is Community?

Key Concept: **Besides being a resident of your city or town and your neighborhood, you are a member of a particular school, a cultural community, and probably one or more clubs or organizations.**

- The people with whom you interact and look to for friendship, information, and social support in all of these different communities make up your **social network.**

- The city or town in which you live has a number of specific features that shape your sense of community.

- Your neighborhood includes the people in the immediate vicinity of your home.

- You form friendships and develop leadership skills in your school community.

- Your cultural background contributes to your sense of community.

- **Community service organizations** are official groups whose members act or unite for a common purpose, such as recreation, learning, and service.

How Communities Affect Health

Key Concept: **Community factors contribute significantly to the physical and social health of community members.**

- Your city or town provides basic health services, health legislation, and promotion of healthy and active lifestyles.

- Some communities promote health through community design. **Mixed-use development** means building homes closer to businesses and schools. Mixed-use development is a healthier alternative to spread-out suburbs, also called **urban sprawl.**

- A neighborhood sometimes organizes safety patrols or sports teams to protect the health of its members.

- At school, many factors affect your health. These include availability of nutritious foods, safe travel routes, violence prevention policies, opportunities for physical activity, and access to health services.

- Your cultural community acts as a "safety net" and strengthens your social health.

- Community service organizations, other volunteer groups, and religious organizations do many things to improve the health of community members.

Section 25-1 Note Taking Guide

Your Community, Your Health (pp. 664–669)

What Is Community?

1. List three benefits of belonging to a social network.

   a. <u>friendship</u>

   b. _____

   c. _____

2. List five kinds of communities to which you belong.

   a. _____

   b. _____

   c. _____

   d. _____

   e. _____

3. Give two examples of community service organizations for teens.

   a. _____

   b. _____

Name _____ Class _____ Date _____

Section 25-1: Note Taking Guide (continued)

How Communities Affect Health

4. Complete the table about how different types of communities affect health. Use the terms from the box below.

| Neighborhood | Cultural community | School community |
| City or town | Community service organizations | |

Community	Contributions to Health
a. _____ _____	provides sewage treatment; enforces laws that limit noise levels; runs food pantries, blood drives, and weight-management groups
b. _____ _____	organizes safety patrols; organizes block parties
c. _____ _____	has policies to protect students; provides students with access to counselors; provides students with opportunities for physical activity
d. _____ _____	can serve as a safety net for members; strengthens social health through shared cultural traditions
e. _____ _____	SADD works to reduce traffic fatalities; scouts organize food drives; religious organizations sponsor youth groups

Chapter 25 Building Health Skills

Locating Community Resources (pp. 670–671)

When you are facing a problem, it helps to know where to find help. Use this worksheet to identify community resources teens can use when they need help.

1. Talk to a trusted adult.

Look at the list below. Think of the adults you know and trust. Write the names of at least three adults you are comfortable talking to.

Parent	
Other relative	
Friend of family	
Trusted teacher	
Coach	
School counselor	
Family doctor	
Religious leader	

2. Search the Internet.

Review Dierdra's story on page 670 of your book. Dierdra is feeling depressed about her parents' divorce.

a. What words might Dierdra put into a search engine to find advice or support?

divorce; _____

_____

b. List two types of organizations she should look for in order to access the most accurate information.

government agencies; _____

_____

Locating Community Resources (continued)

3. Use your local telephone directory.

Again, think about Dierdra's problem. List at least three listings she could check in her local telephone directory for help.

a. <u>Community Health Services</u> _____

b. _____

c. _____

4. Call to find out what services are provided.

Imagine you are Dierdra. You are going to call an organization you identified in your local telephone directory. Outline what you would say when you call. Include both a description of the problem you want to discuss and the information about the organization you want to find out.

<u>I need to talk to someone about my parents' divorce.</u> _____

_____

_____

_____

_____

5. Select one resource and make an appointment to visit.

How would Dierdra choose among the different agencies she called? List at least three things she should consider before making an appointment.

a. <u>Do the hours of the agency fit with my schedule?</u> _____

b. _____

c. _____

Section 25-2 **Summary**

Air Quality and Health (pp. 672–676)

Air Pollution

Key Concept: **Air pollutants can damage the respiratory system, enter the bloodstream and harm other parts of the body, and reduce your protection from the sun's radiation.**

- **Pollution** is the presence or release of substances—called pollutants—into the environment in quantities that are harmful to living organisms.
- One of the biggest sources of air pollution is the burning of **fossil fuels** such as coal, oil, and natural gas.
- **Smog** is a brown haze that forms when air pollutants react in the presence of sunlight.
- The **ozone layer,** located high up in the earth's atmosphere, absorbs most of the harmful ultraviolet light radiated by the sun. It is damaged by pollutants called chloroflourocarbons (klawr oh floor oh KAHR bunz).

Indoor Air Pollution

Key Concept: **Indoor air pollution is most severe in homes and other buildings that have been sealed against air leaks.**

- To reduce pollutant levels, some houses and offices are designed to allow for adequate ventilation year-round.
- **Asbestos** (as BES tus) is a fibrous mineral that was used in fireproofing and other building materials. If inhaled, asbestos fibers can damage the lungs and cause lung cancer. Asbestos is now banned in new construction.
- A naturally occurring gas called **radon** is a serious indoor air pollutant.

Protecting Air Quality

Key Concept: **In addition to government regulations, personal actions, such as your day-to-day decisions about energy use, directly affect air quality.**

- The Clean Air Act of 1970 identified major air pollutants and set standards for air quality.
- Other federal and local government measures can help reduce air pollution.
- Government air quality ratings can help communities monitor their progress toward achieving cleaner, healthier air.
- Steps you can take to help reduce air pollution include walking instead of driving, keeping your vehicle well-maintained, and using appropriate thermostat settings in each season.

Name _____ Class _____ Date _____

Note Taking Guide

Air Quality and Health (pp. 672–676)

Air Pollution

1. List three effects air pollutants can have on the body.

   a. _damage the respiratory system_ _____

   b. _____

   c. _____

2. Put a check mark next to the statement that best describes the effect of CFCs.

   _____ a. CFCs destroy the ozone layer, allowing harmful ultraviolet rays to reach Earth's surface.

   _____ b. CFCs protect the ozone layer by blocking the ultraviolet rays that can cause skin cancer.

3. Complete the table by identifying the major air pollutants.

Pollutant	Health Effect
a. _____	causes nausea and fatigue
b. _____ c. _____ d. _____	aggravates respiratory conditions
e. _____	may irritate throat, nose, lungs, and eyes

Section 25-2: **Note Taking Guide** (continued)

Indoor Air Pollution

4. List five sources of indoor air pollution.

   a. fumes from carpets and paint _____

   b. _____

   c. _____

   d. _____

   e. _____

Protecting Air Quality

5. List three ways the government can help reduce air pollution.

   a. require factories and power plants to install filters to remove

   toxic pollutants _____

   b. _____

   _____

   c. _____

   _____

6. Describe four ways you can help reduce air pollution.

   a. I can walk, ride a bicycle, or use public transportation instead of

   using a car. _____

   b. _____

   _____

   c. _____

   _____

   d. _____

   _____

Name _____ Class _____ Date _____

Protecting Land and Water (pp. 677–683)

Waste Disposal

Key Concept: Hazardous wastes build up in the environment and threaten the health of plants and animals, including humans.

- Waste that can be broken down by microorganisms is called **biodegradable waste.** It does not usually cause pollution.

- A **hazardous waste** is any waste that is either flammable, explosive, corrosive, or toxic to humans or other living things.

- A **landfill** is a permanent storage area where garbage and other wastes are deposited and covered with soil.

- **Recycling** is the process of reclaiming raw materials from discarded products and using them to create new products.

Sources of Water Pollution

Key Concept: Wastes from household, industrial, and agricultural sources can cause pollution of water resources.

- The waste material carried from toilets and drains is referred to as **sewage.** The Clean Water Act requires communities to treat their raw sewage before releasing it into the environment.

- Household cleaners, industrial operations, and agricultural runoff are sources of water pollution.

- **Runoff** is water that drains from land into streams.

Maintaining Environmental Health

Key Concept: Cleaning up waste sites, improving waste management, and conserving natural resources are three solutions for protecting land and water.

- The EPA has placed over 1,000 of the most dangerous hazardous waste sites, called "Superfund" sites, on a national priority list for cleanup.

- Legal dump sites and collection centers for hazardous chemicals prevent wastes from leaking into the environment.

- **Conservation** is the protection and preservation of the natural environment by managing natural resources wisely and developing land for new construction responsibly.

- You can help reduce the problems associated with land and water pollution by following the "three Rs"—reduce, reuse, and recycle.

Section 25-3 Note Taking Guide

Protecting Land and Water (pp. 677–683)

Waste Disposal

1. Complete the graphic organizer about hazardous wastes. Use the words and phrases from the box below.

solvents	mercury	radioactive materials
lead	diseases	developmental problems
birth defects		

Main Idea: Hazardous wastes build up in the environment and threaten the health of plants and animals, including humans.

Include

a. _motor oil_

b. _pesticides_

c. _____

d. _____

e. _____

f. _____

Can Cause

g. _cancer_

h. _____

i. _____

j. _____

2. Put a check mark next to the best definition of *recycling*.

_____ **a.** the process of reclaiming raw materials from discarded products and using them to create new products

_____ **b.** the process of returning old products to purchase new products

Section 25-3: **Note Taking Guide** (continued)

Sources of Water Pollution

3. Complete the table about sources of water pollution. Use the terms from the box below.

| Agricultural runoff | Household cleaners |
| Industrial wastes | Household sewage |

Type of Pollutant	Facts
a. _____ _____	waste material from toilets and drains; contains bacteria and viruses that cause disease
b. _____ _____	some contain phosphates, which harm water plants and animals; some contain chlorine, which is toxic and can create carcinogens
c. _____ _____	may be very hazardous, non-biodegradable, or both; may include lead, cadmium, and mercury
d. _____ _____	often contains chemicals used to control weeds and insects; chemicals may contaminate fish and game animals

Section 25-3: Note Taking Guide (continued)

Maintaining Environmental Health

4. Complete the graphic organizer about ways to promote environmental health.

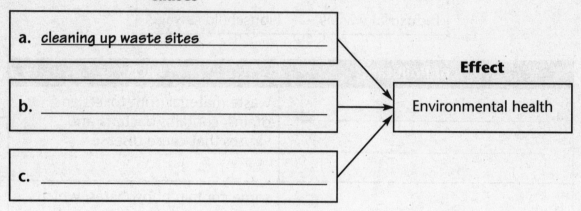

Causes

a. <u>cleaning up waste sites</u>

b. _____

c. _____

Effect

Environmental health

5. Put a check mark next to the "three Rs" that you can follow to reduce water pollution.

_____ **a.** Reduce

_____ **b.** Return

_____ **c.** Reuse

_____ **d.** Recycle

_____ **e.** Repeat

Name _____ Class _____ Date _____

Working for Community Health (pp. 684–688)

A Sense of Community

Key Concept: **Two keys to building a sense of community are civic engagement and a shared vision of the future.**

• The level of involvement that average citizens have in the planning and decision-making that affects their community is called **civic engagement.**

• **Consensus-building** is the process by which a community agrees on a vision for the future. Common goals allow a community to make progress.

• Lack of shared vision may result in fewer investments in school systems, transportation systems, and public health programs.

Getting Involved in Your Community

Key Concept: **There are three steps to getting involved: become informed, volunteer your time, and be an advocate.**

• The first step in getting involved in your community is to become informed about health-related issues and the strengths and weaknesses of the community.

• After you've become informed, the next step is to get more involved.

• More than half of America's teens do an average of four hours per week of volunteer community service work with religious organizations, community service organizations, school groups, and other groups.

• Being an advocate means speaking or writing in support of a person or issue.

• You can advocate for community issues by speaking out at public meetings, writing letters, or communicating with others on the Web.

Name _____ Class _____ Date _____

Note Taking Guide

Working for Community Health (pp. 684–688)

A Sense of Community

1. Complete the concept map about building a sense of community.
   Use the phrases from the box below.

registering to vote when you turn 18	short-term sacrifice for long-term goals
attending public hearings	consensus-building
volunteering in a political campaign	participating in community government

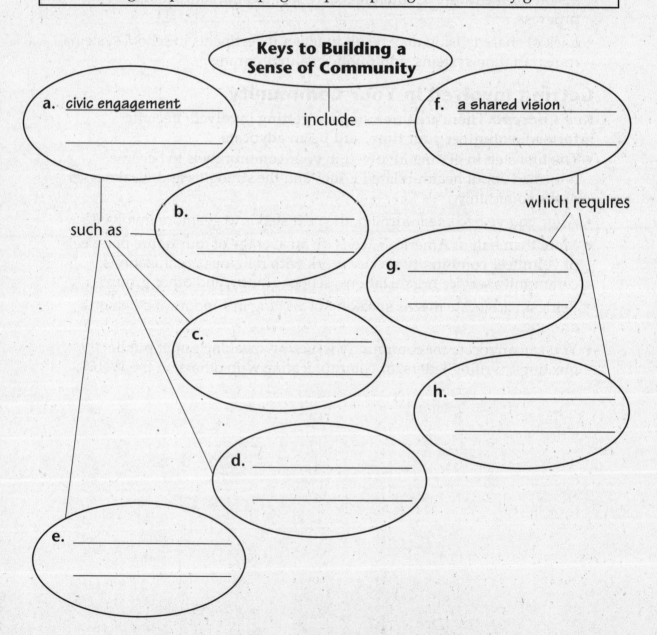

Keys to Building a Sense of Community

a. civic engagement _____

include

f. a shared vision _____

which requires

such as

b. _____

g. _____

c. _____

h. _____

d. _____

e. _____

Name _____ Class _____ Date _____

Section 25-4: **Note Taking Guide** (continued)

Getting Involved in Your Community

2. Complete the flowchart about getting involved in your community.
   Use the sentences from the box below.

   | Be an advocate. | Become informed. | Volunteer your time. |

   a. _____
   Read the local newspaper; interview community leaders.

   ↓

   b. _____
   Food drive; "Meals on Wheels"

   ↓

   c. _____
   Speak out about an issue at public meetings.

Section 26-1 **Summary**

Safety at Home and in Your Community
(pp. 694–701)

What Are Unintentional Injuries?

Key Concept: Five factors that can help prevent unintentional injuries or lessen their damage are awareness, knowledge, ability, state of mind, and environmental conditions.

- An **unintentional injury** is an unplanned injury.
- Recognizing the risks to your safety and knowing what actions to take can reduce the risk of unintentional injury.
- A person who is tired, rushed, or under the influence of alcohol or other drugs has an increased risk of unintentional injury.

Injuries in the Home

Key Concept: Common unintentional injuries that occur in the home are due to falls, poisoning, suffocation, fires, electric shock, and firearms.

- The main way to avoid falls is to focus on environmental conditions.
- Keeping hazardous substances locked in cabinets helps reduce the risk of unintentional poisoning.
- **Flammable materials** catch fire easily and burn quickly. Flammable materials should be stored properly to reduce the risk of fire.
- Death from direct contact with electricity is called **electrocution** (ih lek truh KYOO shun).

Natural Disasters

Key Concept: Earthquakes, tornadoes, hurricanes, floods, blizzards, and many forest fires are examples of natural disasters.

- If a disaster occurs in your area, follow instructions given over the Emergency Alert System.
- You may need to leave home because of a hurricane, flood, or forest fire.

Protecting Yourself From Crime

Key Concept: You can prevent assault or reduce the likelihood of injury by following certain safety guidelines. The most basic guideline is to avoid risky situations.

- An **assault** is an unlawful attempt or threat to harm someone.
- **Rape** means that one person forces another to have sexual relations.
- A **stalker** is someone who makes repeated, unwanted contact with a person and may threaten to kill or injure the person.

Section 26-1 *Note Taking Guide*

Safety at Home and in Your Community
(pp. 694–701)

What Are Unintentional Injuries?

1. List and describe five factors that can help you prevent unintentional injuries.

   a. <u>Awareness: recognize risks to your safety.</u>

   b. <u>Knowledge: know what actions to take.</u>

   c. _____

   d. _____

   e. _____

Injuries in the Home

2. Complete the table about preventing injuries in the home. Use the terms from the box below.

Falls   Electric shock   Unintentional shooting   Poisoning

Injury	Ways to Prevent
a. _____	Keep stairs and walkways uncluttered and well lit. Make sure floors are not slippery.
b. _____	Keep hazardous substances in a locked cabinet. Install carbon monoxide detectors.
c. _____	Never use appliances when you are wet or near water. Place safety covers over unused electrical outlets.
d. _____	Keep firearms unloaded and locked in a place where children cannot reach them. Store ammunition separately.

Section 26-1: **Note Taking Guide** (continued)

3. For each common cause of household fires, list one way you could reduce the risk.

   a. Cooking <u>Keep a fire extinguisher in the kitchen.</u>_____

   b. Smoking _____

   c. Electrical wiring _____

   d. Heating units _____

   e. Flammable materials _____

4. Complete the flowchart about steps to take if your home is on fire. Use the sentences from the box below.

   > Once you are outside, do not go back in.
   >
   > Go to a neighbor's house and call the fire department.
   >
   > If there is a lot of smoke, crawl along the floor to the nearest exit.

   a. <u>Leave immediately.</u>_____

   ↓

   b. _____

   ↓

   c. _____

   ↓

   d. _____

Section 26-1: **Note Taking Guide** (continued)

Natural Disasters

5. Complete the table by matching each guideline with a type of natural disaster. Use the terms from the box below.

| Tornado | Flood | Blizzard | Earthquake | Hurricane | Forest fire |

Disaster	Safety Guideline
a. _____	If you are indoors, stand under the frame of an interior door or crawl under a table.
b. _____	Go to the lowest floor of your home. Keep some windows open but stay away from windows.
c. _____	Place tape across windows and board them up.
d. _____	Before evacuating, turn off your home's water, gas, and electricity.
e. _____	Stay inside your home or other warm structure.
f. _____	Listen to local authorities if they tell you to evacuate an area at risk for fire.

Protecting Yourself From Crime

6. List one safety guideline to follow in each situation.

a. Home alone Lock all doors and windows._____

b. Driving _____

_____

c. Car breaks down _____

_____

d. Someone tries to rob you _____

_____

e. See crime in progress _____

_____

Section 26-2 ## Summary

Safety at Work and Play (pp. 702–709)

Occupational Safety

Key Concept: **Many occupational injuries and illnesses can either be prevented or made less serious by removing potential hazards from the workplace.**

- An **occupational injury** is any wound or damage to the body that results from an event in the work environment.

- An **occupational illness** is any abnormal condition or disorder caused by exposure to the work environment.

- It is the responsibility of your employer to keep your workplace as safe as possible and to tell you about any on-the-job hazards.

- It is your responsibility to be well rested and alert, to be sober, and to follow all safety procedures.

- When working on a farm, it is important to be properly trained on equipment and to use common sense.

Recreational Safety

Key Concept: **Whatever recreational activities you enjoy, you should follow four basic safety guidelines.**

- Learn and apply the proper skills.

- Have appropriate, well-maintained equipment.

- Know the safety rules specific to the activity.

- Prepare adequately for the activity.

- **Survival floating** is a lifesaving technique that allows you to float and breathe without using energy.

- **Active supervision** means that you keep children in your view at all times when they are in or near the water.

- To reduce the risk of recreational injury when boating, take a boating safety class and always wear an approved personal flotation device (PFD).

- The overturning of a boat is called **capsizing.**

- Never drink alcohol or use other drugs when you are going to be swimming or boating.

- Always wear protective gear when playing a contact sport.

- When riding a bicycle or recreational vehicle, always wear proper safety equipment, including a helmet. Never ride under the influence of alcohol or other drugs.

Name _____ Class _____ Date _____

Section 26-2 Note Taking Guide

Safety at Work and Play (pp. 702–709)

Occupational Safety

1. Complete the graphic organizer with details about occupational safety.

Main Idea: Many occupational injuries and illnesses can be either prevented or made less serious by removing potential hazards from the workplace.

Teen Workers

Farm Safety

a. Employer's responsibility

_____

_____

b. Your responsibility

_____

_____

c. Never operate equipment

_____

_____ .

d. To protect eyes and ears, wear

_____

_____ .

Recreational Safety

2. List four basic safety guidelines you should follow during recreational activities.

   a. <u>Learn and apply the proper skills.</u>_____

   b. _____

   c. _____

   d. _____

3. List four things you should take with you when hiking or camping.

   a. <u>first-aid kit</u>_____   c. _____

   b. _____   d. _____

Section 26-2: **Note Taking Guide** (continued)

4. Compare water safety and boating safety by completing the Venn diagram. Write similarities where the circles overlap, and differences on the left and right sides.

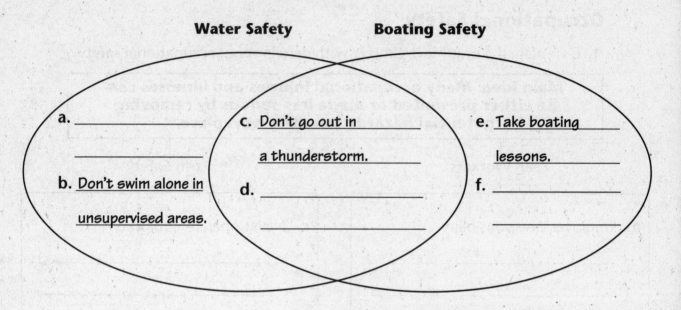

Water Safety   **Boating Safety**

a. _____

_____

b. Don't swim alone in

unsupervised areas.

c. Don't go out in _____

a thunderstorm.

d. _____

_____

e. Take boating _____

lessons.

f. _____

_____

5. Compare sports safety and bicycle safety by completing the Venn diagram. Write similarities where the circles overlap, and differences on the left and right sides.

Sports Safety   **Bicycle Safety**

a. Drink lots of _____

water. _____

b. _____

c. Wear protective _____

clothing. _____

d. _____

_____

e. _____

_____

f. Signal your _____

intentions.

Chapter 26 **Building Health Skills**

Analyzing Risks and Benefits (pp. 710–711)

Making responsible decisions is a sign of maturity. It shows that you are beginning to take control of your own well-being. Use this worksheet to help you learn to analyze risks and benefits before you make a decision.

1. **Identify the possible risks involved in taking this action.**

    A risk is a possible harmful outcome or consequence of taking a certain action. Think of a decision you have faced where physical injury was a possible risk. When you made your decision, which of these steps did you follow?

I identified all the possible negative consequences.	Yes	No
I determined if any of the negative consequences were likely to cause a serious injury.	Yes	No
I rated the likelihood of each consequence actually happening.	Yes	No

2. **Identify the possible benefits of taking this action.**

    Once you have identified the negative consequences of an action, what should you do next?

    a. _____

    _____

    b. _____

    _____

Analyzing Risks and Benefits (continued)

3. Determine what you could do to reduce the risk of injury.

There are ways to reduce the degree of risk involved and maximize the benefits. Describe how each of the factors listed could help someone prevent unintentional injuries. You can use examples from decisions you have faced.

a. Knowledge and awareness _____

_____

b. Ability _____

_____

c. State of mind _____

_____

d. Environmental decisions _____

_____

4. Determine if the benefits outweigh the risks.

Think again about a decision you faced where physical injury was a possible risk. When you made your decision, which of these steps did you follow?

I asked myself if the benefits outweighed the risks.	Yes	No
I thought of strategies for reducing the risk of injury.	Yes	No

Summary

Motor Vehicle Safety (pp. 712–715)

Automobile Safety

Key Concept: You can be a safe driver, regardless of your age. To be a safe driver, you need to practice good driving skills and know how to respond to risky situations.

- Drivers between the ages of 15 and 24 are involved in more motor vehicle crashes than any other age group because they lack driving experience and tend to take more risks.

- Alcohol affects a person's self-control and judgment, slows reaction time, blurs vision, and reduces coordination.

- There are risk factors that you can control when you are driving or riding in a car.

- Some risk factors that come with driving are outside of your control, such as road construction and bad weather.

- **Defensive driving** means that you constantly monitor other drivers around you, and do not assume they will do what you think they should do. Defensive driving allows you to avoid hazardous situations.

- **Road rage** is dangerous or violent behavior by a person who becomes angry or frustrated while driving. Stay away from drivers you suspect might have road rage.

School Bus Safety

Key Concept: When riding in a school bus, there are rules you should follow to ensure everybody's safety.

- Stay seated on the bus at all times.

- Avoid fighting and arguing. Do not throw things. These behaviors distract the bus driver.

- Watch for cars when getting off the bus and crossing the street.

- Drivers should always stop when a school bus's stop sign swings out and its red lights are flashing. This allows students exiting the bus to cross the street safely.

Section 26-3   Note Taking Guide

Motor Vehicle Safety (pp. 712–715)

Automobile Safety

1. List four safety guidelines for risk factors you can control while driving.

   a. <u>Take a course in driver education.</u> _____

   b. _____

   c. _____

   d. _____

2. List four parts of a vehicle that must be in good working condition to reduce the risk of crashes.

   a. <u>brakes</u> _____ c. _____

   b. _____ d. _____

3. List two safety guidelines for driving with each of the following risk factors.

   a. Construction zone <u>Slow down. Obey the lower posted speed limit.</u>

   _____

   b. Low visibility _____

   _____

   c. Slippery road _____

   _____

School Bus Safety

4. List four rules you should follow when riding in a school bus.

   a. <u>Stay seated at all times.</u> _____

   b. _____

   c. _____

   d. _____